BUG

BUG

*Deaf Identity and
Internal Revolution*

Christopher Jon Heuer

Gallaudet University Press
Washington, DC

Gallaudet University Press
Washington, DC 2002
http://gupress.gallaudet.edu

© 2007 by Gallaudet University Press
All rights reserved. Published 2007
Printed in the United States of America

Library of Congress Cataloging-in-Publication Data
Heuer, Christopher Jon.
  Bug : deaf identity and internal revolution / Christopher Jon Heuer.
    p. cm.
  ISBN-13: 978-1-56368-357-2 (alk. paper)
  I. Title.
  PS3608.E89B84 2007
  818'.609—dc22

                                    2007014122

∞ The paper used in this publication meets the minimum
requirements of American National Standard for Information
Sciences—Permanence of Paper for Printed Library Materials,
ANSI Z39.48-1984.

This book is dedicated to the spirit of Saul D. Alinsky.

Contents

Hence the saying:
If you know the enemy and know yourself,
you need not fear the result of a hundred battles. . . .
Sun Tzu—*The Art of War*

Foreword

John Lee Clark

What you have in your hands is a bomb. But it is the kind you need to hold on to for dear life, not run away from. For this reason, this book is already a classic.

The Nobel Prize in literature laureate J. M. Coetzee once defined a classic as a work that a community cannot afford to lose. I knew right away that *Bug* would be something the Deaf world needed when, sitting with me on the steps outside of my apartment building on a lovely afternoon in early August, Christopher Jon Heuer signed under my listening hand: "My book: Every essay me write, me try my best do what? Piss off someone!" This may seem like a shallow object for writing a book, pissing people off—a crude gimmick. But it is not. It is a noble goal that, if accomplished, will let the Deaf world grow. I write *let* instead of *make* because no one can make anything so magical as growth happen in someone else. But one can provide all of what is needed for growth.

The most important thing this book does to promote growth is to make *room* for that growth. How can anything grow if it doesn't have room to grow? The essays in this book are important and have explosive value because there is so little space for growth in the Deaf world. What I mean is that, to be a member of the Deaf community, you have to be audiologically deaf, a fluent signer, and preferably a graduate of a school for the Deaf.

For you to access the highest social standing and positions of leadership, you have to come from a Deaf family—the more generations of unbroken Deaf lineage, the better. You don't *really* have to be all of that, but the community is structured so that you have more to overcome the less you fit the criteria.

Now, this model of what a Deaf person should be was absolutely necessary. For centuries, Deaf people have internalized mainstream society's belief that they are inherently inferior beings. Deaf people have been utter outcasts; deaf babies were thought to be unworthy of life and were thrown into rivers. Despite the pride Deaf people instinctively took in their sign languages, they were uncertain whether these were legitimate, bona fide languages until the latter part of the twentieth century. So the Deaf Pride movement *had* to establish an ideology complete with the community's idea of the perfect Deaf person, or as we say in American sign, "Deaf strong."

There is no one at fault for this, but there was one crucial weakness in this ideology, which is primarily concerned with identity: It failed to take into account that Deaf culture and what is generally known as the Deaf community are two different things. Deaf culture is only one group among many true components of a diverse and inclusive community. But Deaf culture became the standard for the rest of the community, a standard that was often simply impossible for members of other cultures and groups in the community to meet. After the Deaf Pride movement's crowning historical moment—the Deaf President Now protest at Gallaudet University in 1988; then The Deaf Way, the first international festival celebrating Deaf culture in 1989; followed by the passage in 1990 of the Americans with Disabilities Act, amidst many other smaller revolutions—the community found itself diving headfirst into a boiling cauldron of an identity crisis. What about all of those young people who were the products of mainstreaming programs at public schools and who now constituted the majority of the Deaf population? What about the Black Deaf people and other Deaf people with different and relevant ethnic ties that make them distinct from Deaf White people? What about the hearing children of Deaf adults who are so torn between two worlds, between what is in their hearts and warring expectations imposed on them? What about someone like me, who was born Deaf but became blind, finding that I no longer fit in fully with sighted Deaf people and yet am still a part of "their" community? What about someone like Christopher Jon Heuer, who mouths too much, who graduated from a public school, who at times wears hearing aids, whose hearing wife signs better than he does . . . all the while being someone who cares, probably too much, about Deaf people, who believes passionately in Deaf equality and in the value of American sign in the education of Deaf children, and whose heart quite simply bleeds more for the love of Deaf people than that of anyone else I know?

All of them are members of the community, but all of them feel like misfits. Why? Because there is no room for them in the leading ideology of the so-called Deaf community. What defines a culturally Deaf person is, as it should be, the purview of Deaf culture, which has its own exclusive values. But this ideology has been so powerful as to extend its limiting forces all around it in the larger community. Christopher Jon Heuer has written this book hoping to destroy such forces, dropping a bomb into the landscape of the signing community. But it will not detonate by itself. Only readers can do that, by responding to the words in this book.

That is why Heuer's modus operandi is an earnest and sustained attempt to piss someone off, because that will trigger a reaction. For every pissed-off reader, there is going to be a reader weeping for joy, so happy to find that she is not alone and that she is not crazy for being who she is. Heuer's main concern is not whether someone hates him or loves him, but that the explosive materials he offers detonate, opening new space where the community, in all of its parts and as a whole, can advance to the next age in its long and embattled, but proud, history. It is because of this that many readers will try to dismiss Heuer as a radical. Deaf people will do this for different reasons than hearing people, but the primary reason people will dismiss Heuer is because they are afraid of change.

Heuer is a radical only in the sense that he is doing what should have been done a long time ago. That is all. He is not extreme in any other regard. Hearing people have found justification in trying to eradicate the Deaf "variety of the human race." They have forbidden Deaf people from signing. They have said that signing is wrong and that speaking is right, and that all Deaf people must speak. They have sought to make deaf children as like hearing people as much as possible. You will not find anything remotely similar in reverse; that is, Deaf people as a group have never imposed their will on hearing people, nor have they ever been in a position to do so. Heuer does not say that hearing people should be wiped out. He does not say that all hearing people should sign. He does not say that hearing children should be deafened by every possible means and made to be upstanding citizens of the Deaf world. In light of this, even Heuer's strongest opinions are excruciatingly sensible, his points the very picture of reason.

But his words—the way he proposes his ideas—are a whole different matter. He does everything in his power to make every word inflammable. He has to do this to get through the murk of apathy and uncertainty that pervades much social thought in the community today. He knows there are flames raging deep inside each and every Deaf person, and his greatest gift to them in writing this book is bringing new ideas, new perspectives, and new strong and sure signs as close to the flame as he can. The rest is up to you, the reader. It does not matter if you are Deaf, are a signer, or have nothing to do with our community, and it does not matter in what way you respond; however, the reader's response is what we cannot afford to lose.

Acknowledgments

Many of these essays were originally published in my "Man on the Street" column for *The Tactile Mind Weekly*. I would like to thank John and Adrean Clark of The Tactile Mind Press for their steadfast friendship, guidance, and support. You and *TTMW* will be in my heart forever.

Several other essays were originally published in my "Mind over Matter" column for the National Association of the Deaf—Members Only Area's website. Therefore I'd also like to thank Shane Feldman and the NAD for the opportunity to write for them!

Under-the-table thanks go to the notorious Agent M (you know who you are) for her deep literary analysis. If tortured, I promise not to reveal your name until they bring out the jumper cables.

Much thanks to Sara Caroline Finklea, Alison Aubrecht, Justin Small, Tiri Fellows, and Amanda Clark—in exactly that mysterious and nonalphabetical order—for their editing and feedback. If we haven't had enough beer by the time this book hits deadline, I owe you all yet another one.

Special thanks to Tarra Grammenos for being the Late Stuff Read-It Girl.

Thanks also to Nat and Rachel Davour for the awesome cover art! If not for the cockroach, would this book have come to be? Maybe, but then it might have been called *Porn* or something.

I would also like to thank my wife Amy for her unwavering devotion (which she showed by allowing herself, countless times, to be dragged into my office to "read just one more thing"). Love ya, babe.

Last but not least, thank you Gallaudet University Press for letting *Bug* crawl into the light of day!

BUG

Introduction

On Small Things Easily Squished
(and Alternative Destinies)

In March 2003, my good friend John Lee Clark asked me if I would be willing to write a column about whatever was bugging me that week.

Well . . . that's not exactly true. The publication I would write for was to be called *The Tactile Mind Weekly* (*TTMW*)— so yes, the column had to be a weekly one. But John never actually specified that my column had to be about something that was "bugging" me. All he really said was that it had to be about deafness. But you see, to me, those two things were one and the same. Lots of things bugged me about deafness. A lot of things still do.

Before I go on, though, I'd like to qualify those last two statements. When I was growing up, my mother's response to every problem I had was: "Well, he just needs to adjust to his deafness." Believe me, I do mean *every* problem. Bloody nose? "Chris, you need to adjust to your deafness." Homework not done? "I know it's hard adjusting to your deafness, honey, but. . . ." Acne scarring? "Lots of teenagers get zits, Chris. I know it's hard for you, dealing with this while trying to adjust to your. . . ."

On and on this went—for years. One day, I got sick of it. I don't really know how the argument got started, but I ended up banging my fist on the table and shouting, "Ma, stop!" Stop, because it's not your deafness that spits in your ear and slaps you upside the back of your head as it runs past you in the hallways of mainstream schools. It doesn't talk down to you, treat you like a Retard, or leave you sitting at the family dinner table, neglected and alone, in the presence of oblivious, yapping multitudes.

Other people do that.

Thus my intention was to kick a little ass in my column. I was mad, and Hearing America has had it coming for years. It's not easy, trying to tell them off. The problem isn't the argument. It's the audience. The ability to hear is not the same thing as the ability to listen. Brutal truths are painful and therefore threatening. Avoidance is easier. Denial is easier. "Stop feeling sorry for yourself" is easier. Their only alternative is acknowledging their part in the problem.

On the other hand, Deaf culture isn't exactly a shining beacon of hope either. Although not all Deaf people adhere to the same values, more than a few subscribe to some pretty exclusionary ones. Amongst them seem to be these: If . . .

1. you weren't born to Deaf parents
2. you didn't attend a Deaf institution (bonus points if you were actually born in one of the dorms)
3. your ASL is not as crisp as a freshly sliced apple

. . . then you are not worth the saliva required to spit in your face.

Meanwhile literacy rates among huge numbers of deaf high school graduates—orally or manually educated—remain at fourth-grade levels, as they have for decades. Relatively few Deaf education teachers can sign at expert or even adequate levels. Cochlear implants are a hair away from being programmed to raise deaf children with no parental involvement whatsoever (from a marketing viewpoint, why mess with historical trends?). In the midst of all of that, is there anything poignant an overwhelmed columnist can write?

For what it's worth, I tried. "The Man on the Street" ran in *TTMW* for around two years. You'll soon be reading the best of those columns right here in this book (*I* thought they were pretty good, anyway . . . decide for yourself)!

Before you do, though, a couple more things:

One, only 60 percent of *Bug* is composed of what used to be "Man on the Street" columns (all revised, polished, and converted into essays). Another 10 percent of the essays come from an entirely different column, a monthly one that I wrote for the National Association of the Deaf's online Members Only Area (NAD-MOA). That one was called "Mind over Matter." I wrote for the NAD for about as long as I wrote for *TTMW*, meaning that, for a while, I was writing both columns simultaneously (and very nearly burned myself out doing so). That's where the variation in the length of the essays comes from. I was sharing *TTMW* space with anywhere from five to nine or more writers, depending on the issue. We generally liked to keep things shorter over there. NAD-MOA, on the other hand, had fewer columnists and a lot more room to ramble.

Two, many of the poems in *Bug* come from an earlier book of poetry that I wrote for The Tactile Mind Press entitled *All Your Parts Intact*. Trust me; this isn't a sneaky attempt on my part to get you to buy two books' worth of identical material. I make it a practice to reprint a couple of poems from my older books in my newer books. That way if I ever become a Banned Writer (keep your fingers crossed), no singular book burning will wipe out all of my stuff.

Three, the remainder of the material in *Bug* is all new. This is why you're paying for the book. It's called capitalism. I like capitalism. It will help me retire, after which point I'll probably stop writing books. Therefore if you don't like my new stuff, by paying to read it, you're ironically enough helping me to the endpoint of my literary career, where you'll never have to hear from me again. It's a win-win situation.

Four, the intended audience for this book changes from essay to essay and from poem to poem. Deal with this. I tried to group things together loosely based on themes, but I'm a weird person who writes about weird things, so this wasn't easy. Furthermore, you're also going to have to make sense of the following system: A capital "D" in these essays usually denotes membership in the Deaf culture, while a lower-case "d" denotes those who are biologically deaf, yet have chosen not to join the Deaf culture. At times, the line between these two groups of D/deaf people will blur, and at times, that's as deliberate on my part as it is unintentional. If it seems that the various essays overlap, and even become contradictory, I ask for your patience. You, too, are full of overlapping and contradictory messages. If you doubt this, get your closest friends drunk and ask them what they really think of you.

And finally, five: Where does the title of this book come from? About a year into my writing "Man on the Street," people began nodding at me as we passed each other in the hallowed halls of Gallaudet. My fame never quite reached the point where people started buying me beers at Deaf Professional Happy Hour (nudge to audience), but that's okay. I'll settle for the nods. At heart, at least, I'm a man of the street. I know exactly what I look like from the scholarly heights of the ivory tower: a bug (synonym for pest; synonym for a small thing easily squished). So be it. I resign myself to my destiny.

Understand something, though. Most people no doubt believe that the destiny of a bug is to become a dime-sized bloodstain on the palm of somebody's hand. But the bug himself?

He believes it's his destiny to start an infestation.

I Choose the Green Crayon

When I quit my job at _____ Bank nine years ago, they tried to process me out with the following questionnaire:

1. Why are you leaving _____ Bank?

Possible answers:

( ) I am taking a new job
( ) I am continuing with my education

. . . and so on. Each question had about four possible answers—and each answer had its own corresponding oval. You were supposed to darken whatever oval you thought fit best.

I said I would only fill out the form if they let me do it in green crayon.

The _____ Bank people were first confused, then annoyed, then confused again. "No," they said. I had to use a #2 pencil. "Simply fill in the ovals that best answer the..."

I insisted on using a green crayon.

Exasperation soon turned to anger (and possibly fear). Desktops were slapped.

"#2 pencil!"

Green crayon!

"Just fill in the ovals!"

Green crayon!

"No!"

Yes!

When it got to within three minutes of closing time (I had shown up at noon), they finally let me go. Not a single corresponding oval was darkened.

Why make such a big deal out of it?

In order to interview for the job, I filled out an application (a form). During the interview, someone read from that form. Now I wanted to leave, and what did they need? Another form! From beginning to end—I was never more to them than a piece of paper! Worse yet, there was no oval for "Other;" no section for listing my own *actual,* honest-to-God reasons for quitting _____ Bank. To this day, I can't get past my outrage long enough to tell anybody what they were. It's the *principle* of the thing; forcing me go through all of that trouble, yet they didn't even care about what I had to say! They wanted me to select from among only *their* answers. There wasn't any room in their petty little _____ Bank brains for *mine!*

I am not anti-Establishment. I am not anti-authority. I am not immature or arrogant or unprofessional. I do not think I'm better than everyone else, and I don't think I deserve special treatment.

I am also not a piece of paper, nor am I somebody else's preconceived answer. I am more. What's the point of writing this book, of looking at deafness in new ways, if everyone has already made up their minds to process me out with corresponding ovals? What's the point in living your life at all if the only thoughts you're allowed to express are the ones deemed acceptable by _____ Bank?

That's not life.

That's a gray cubicle complete with fluorescent lights (#1 cause of eyeball cancer) and granite-colored carpets.

Bald Men Grow Hair When They Want To

Now you see; I'm bald, *and* I'm Bald.

You could teach Continental Drift Theory using my scalp as a globe. The hair that grows on the left side of my head (count the cultivated sideburn) is the jutting peninsula of Florida. The hair on the right is Africa, and that vast expanse of peachy flesh in the middle is the mighty Atlantic. Throw in the isolated island of fuzz above my forehead and you've got Antarctica.

There are a lot of similarities between baldness and deafness, as well as their corresponding cultural identities of Baldness and Deafness. For one thing, in both cases, my acceptance of my hair loss was about as gradual as the onset of my hearing loss.

The fear is the same, too. Hearing parents face the looming specter of cochlear implants—balding men are faced with the looming specter of hair plug transplants. Both cost small fortunes (I checked). And you know how insurance companies give you a lot of shit over the price tag of your new hearing aids? Well, they don't cover Rogaine either. And while I never bothered to try Propecia, I'll bet you a beer they screw you on that one, too.

Of course baldness in newborns is not generally seen as something to freak out over. I don't think the stock from Toupees for Tots would do very well on Wall Street. The biological condition of deafness, on the other hand, is not met with similar parental mellowness. If the kid *stayed* bald, it might be a different story.

Cochlear implant surgery on deaf children two years old and younger has been on the upswing for quite a while now. The Deaf culture, needless to say, isn't exactly thrilled with the trend. But do you notice how nobody ever says anything about those d/Deaf adults who decide, of their own free will, to get one when they become adults? Here we return to the similarities between deaf and bald men. Whether your aim is an implant or a transplant, what difference does it make if you become old enough to decide for yourself that you want one, *but still can't afford the damned thing!* A lot of bald guys can't even pay their membership dues in the proverbial American Hair Club for Men. Meanwhile your mail order K-Mart toupee looks like something the cat coughed up.

The cheaper way out of the "problem" (sarcasm!) is to simply go Bald. Being Bald is being bald with attitude. You shave the pesky topical, back, and side stuff off; grow a satanic goatee to balance out the weight distribution; and, if you've really got guts, put a tattoo of a skull or something on the back of your neck. Kids used to run up to me and say I look like the wrestler Stone Cold. I'd growl and reply, "Screw that, *he* looks like *me.*" I've had this cut for over a decade—dating back to those ancient days when heavy metal hair bands like Motley Crue and Def Leppard were still popular. I don't copy anybody, dude; not even 300-pound professional wrestlers.

Just don't tell them I said that.

Being Bald is great for the bar scene. The small "b" bald guys are always standing in the shadows pawing nervously at their comb-overs. Meanwhile, Bald guys are strutting around like they own the place, casting "Yo, got your back, bro!" nods toward the other Bald guys. Conversation around the pool tables consists of an uneasy mixture of bald guys asking Bald guys about the proper care of razor nicks, and Bald guys asking bald guys if Propecia really grows anything besides marsh grass.

The whole thing can leave you with the assumption that Bald guys occupy the top of the cultural and social food chain in that particular minority. I beg to differ. Each group faces a somewhat common dilemma. A bald guy has to look in the mirror and decide if he's actually the walking medical malady the hot blonde by the bar thinks he is. A Bald guy, though, has to look in the mirror and decide what he's going to do on days when he's too tired to shave, or when his skull tattoo doesn't go with his ass-kicking Armani business suit.

What do you do in those moments when your life has come down to deciding for yourself what you're going to be, instead of letting everybody else decide for you? It's not easy. Bald or bald . . . stand under a bright light, friend, and one way or another, you are going to *reflect*.

I don't know about you, but personally I stopped worrying about it all. When I feel like shaving, I do, and when I don't, I don't. Sometimes I walk around with two or three days' worth of stubble all over my head. Bald guys look at me like I'm some kind of traitor. I snarl quietly at them, and they back down, confused by my challenge to the established social order. So do the Deaf ones. And so, for that matter, does everyone else.

I'm through avoiding bright lights. I stand where I feel like standing.

The "Must Put Pickle" Mentality

Nine restaurants out of ten, it never fails.

"No pickle, please," I'll tell them. I can say this in English, German, and Spanish. I can convey it in complex or simple mime motions. I've written it down. I've drawn little pictures of pickles on my napkin and slashed big "Xs" through them. Once I even tried coloring the pickle (and the "X") for greater visual impact.

Nothing works. The teen waitress in pigtails and braids still brings me my cheeseburger with big fat juicy pickles forming a slime-green puddle under my fries. The college kid with orange hair still hands me my turkey and cheese on wheat with pickle slices cleverly stuffed between the tomatoes and onions. Once I even ordered meatloaf from a rather severe looking grand-mother-type at a roadside mom-n-pop deli. It arrived hot and steaming, pickles pinned to its sides with evil-looking little toothpicks.

Now I'd like to make something clear: I do not have the body type one would normally associate with that of a finicky eater. I eat my chocolate with or without nuts. I drink milk types A through D without complaint. Pickles, though, are another matter entirely. I simply cannot get near them. I shudder at even the faintest wisp of their odor.

However, that's all I do. I don't grimace; I don't gag. I don't become loud or obnoxious and demand that all pickles in a given restaurant be bagged, barreled, and sealed prior to my arrival. I don't make a spectacle of myself. I don't throw things at the chefs. Ask anyone—I'm a quiet man who likes quiet tables. There is absolutely no logical reason thousands of food service employees across the country should pick *me* to pick on over and over again.

So why, in God's great and echoing name, can I not get a pickle-free meal anywhere in the forty-eight states of the American mainland? The whole thing has gotten so bad I'm actually *afraid* to travel to Hawaii or Alaska. I maintain my sanity by believing there's somewhere in the world I could go to order cooked pineapple or sautéed caribou flank and not have these items arrive with a miniature pickle smiley face staring up at me from the plate.

You know . . . I think the associations between some things are just too deeply ingrained into the human psyche for us to ever make much of a dent in the link. Ice cream and cones. Green Bay Packers and Cheese Heads. *Starsky and Hutch.*

Deafness and illiteracy. Deafness and Social Security moochers. Deafness and the Betterment of the Cochlear Implant Industry.

You see, there's that . . . mentality: "Must Put Pickle." They *have* to put it there, period, or physical withdrawal symptoms ensue. This is why the food service industry has such a high turnover rate. When its chefs and waitresses dare to dream of a world without pickles, they immediately get the shakes and start dropping all the plates. The laws of natural selection almost guarantee that anyone still working in a diner after three years is not going to be able to process your diagrams (colored or not) of pickles with "Xs" drawn through them.

Likewise you'll also find the mother who firmly believes her deaf son's illiteracy is caused by his deafness and not by her own refusal to learn to sign. You'll find the Deaf education teacher who believes her students' poor comprehension skills are caused by their deafness and not her own poor teaching and low expectations. You'll find the audiologist who is never going to recommend that parents turn down cochlear implants, because deafness is what causes an overwhelming isolation from social life, and a cochlear implant is the only thing that will save deaf kids.

But try not to let this discourage you too much.

If you can learn to walk into a restaurant and expect the pickle no matter what, it isn't too much of a leap to talk with a nonsigning parent and expect absolutely no acknowledgment of reality no matter what. Just as you can learn to carry along a napkin and mop up the damage being done to your fries, so too can you learn to carry on and mop up the damage being done to deaf children.

Campfires in Boxer Shorts— Confessions of a Hearing Aid-Less Exhibitionist

Herein lay the dilemma: It's after midnight. I want to have a campfire in the semi-privacy of my own backyard, two-thirds of which is relatively well hidden by shrubbery from the sidewalk (which is about twenty yards distant). I'm downstairs in my boxer shorts, because that's the kind of man I am—someone who tramps around after midnight in his underwear. I tramp around in the morning, at noon, and at suppertime in my underwear too, if I feel like it; but that's neither here nor there.

Now, do I creak my way up the stairs to my dresser and put on *real* shorts—possibly awakening my beautiful sleeping wife in the process—or do I skip it? After all, from twenty yards out (and with all of the passersby after midnight being drunk anyway), in the light of a small campfire, my dark navy blue boxer shorts are going to look pretty much just like my dark navy blue *real* shorts. So what's the big deal?

It's kind of stupid that this should even bother me. The truth is that I've *already* sat by numerous backyard campfires in my boxer shorts and absolutely nothing has come of it. Cops have actually walked by and waved (granted I waved at them first) without arresting me for indecent exposure. Neighbors have smiled after I gave them a complimentary tip of my beer can. I've written epic poems in the air with the glowing ends of burning pine branches, and nobody has published them yet. In fact, if I weren't now taking the time to confess that I've just come back inside from having a backyard campfire in my boxer shorts, you never would have even known!

Nonetheless, I feel guilty. I'm a bad citizen. The sleeping children have a right to be safe from the likes of me. Regardless of the fact that, after midnight, visibility in my backyard drops to nothing, and the dim, flickering, orange light of a campfire doesn't really improve on that, I'm nonetheless sure that somewhere, somehow, my iniquity has offended somebody on principle alone. A grown man, beer in hand, lounging around his backyard in his boxer shorts! My word! My mug shot should be taped to every telephone pole within five miles! The world has a right to know! There are laws in this country! If one person breaks the rules, pretty soon everyone will start breaking the rules, and the next thing you know, we'll have teenage girls prancing around in low-riders and thongs!

All I can say is I'm sorry. I guess I'm a born anarchist at heart. Growing up, I never wore my hearing aids when I was supposed to either. If it makes you feel any better, *that* was an infraction I never got away with. In fact, my high school interpreter would yell at me in front of all my friends every time I showed up in class without them on. She'd hiss and ask me what good they were doing me, stuck in a box at home in the back of my desk drawer. Humiliating! She screwed me up! Flattened my self-esteem to the paltry height of an eggless pancake! And now I've grown up into . . . this! A lazy, exhibitionist hoodlum with no regard for anyone other than his sleeping wife!

Disgusting!

Pushed into Faith Healing

Long ago, I was dating this Christian woman, Sandy. In my own defense, let me say three things: (1) She was hot (I have my wife's permission to tell you this, by the way); (2) I was a spankin' new college freshman at UW-Milwaukee, and was opening myself up to new dating experiences; and (3) she struggled enough with her piety to make our relationship interesting.

Nonetheless, she did try to assuage her guilt (and I guess what she thought was *mine*) by taking me to some of the weirdest churches I have ever been to. I am a solid, German-stock Lutheran. The churches I had attended up to that point were on the morose side—Jesus Factories of stained mahogany with an Old Testament emphasis. You know the type . . . stand up, sit down, cue solemn organ music. I'm going to hell, you're going to hell, let's sing a song. . . .

This church, though—wow, man! People were spinning in the aisles. A woman in our pew started having what looked like a seizure and fell to the floor. I couldn't make out what she was saying. I was ready to kneel down to start CPR when Sandy restrained me. She explained later that the woman had been overcome by the Spirit and was now speaking in tongues. In a way, I was oddly relieved. For once in my life, someone sounded like she was speaking in gibberish because she actually *was* speaking in gibberish.

Anyway, the service progressed, and after a while it was time for the faith healing segment. The pastor-slash-tent revivalist asked the "sick" to step up and receive the Spirit (presumably the same one that was causing seizures in the woman lying at my feet). I hesitated, unsure of what to do. I wasn't that into Deaf culture just yet—so I wasn't well-versed in the whole "minority vs. pathology" argument. It just didn't seem polite to refuse. People were staring at me expectantly . . . and somewhat hungrily.

So I went up to the front of the church. I was instantly seized by the revivalist's henchmen: Two guys in suits presumably there to catch me after the Spirit tackled my knees. Only they really weren't. Within seconds, each had a firm grip on my arm, and I realized their *actual* job was to keep me from changing my mind and backing out of the deal. The revivalist placed his hands over my ears—thankfully he had seen Sandy signing to me, so I didn't have to explain what I needed "healed"—and shouted. *He* might have been speaking in tongues, too. We'll never know.

I felt his arms tense up. Before I knew what was happening, he pulled my head to his chest, shouted something, and then forcefully pushed me backwards. The henchmen, on cue, pulled back on my arms (one of them blocked my heel with his foot to speed the process along). You've never seen a smoother group takedown this side of *Cops*. Bam, down I went, face flushed and brow wrinkled. I had to blink back the tears that suddenly formed in my eyes . . . not because I could miraculously hear again, but because when the revivalist yanked my face into his chest, I banged my nose on his crucifix-reinforced breastbone.

What happened next? Not much. I got up and went back to my pew. People continued to look at me expectantly. But by the end of the service I was still deaf, and by the end of the day I was still deaf, and by the end of the week, well. . . .

Sandy and I eventually broke up. Maybe she took it as a lack of faith on my part—the fact that the laying-on-of-hands "cure" didn't take. I don't know—maybe not.

That was hardly the only evidence that I wasn't a Christian of her caliber.

Deaf Man Killed by Flying Golf Ball—A Eulogy of Small Accomplishments

He was a man of accomplishment. Despite
his deafness people would have sworn
he could part the oceans with his hands,
or at least build damned fine birdhouses.

His grandparents loved him, and so did
his grandparent's friends. He earned
a "C+" in math and a "B" in English.
His alcoholic mother with big boobs

kept all of his high school wrestling newspaper
clippings. He was meant to go places;
his high school could not have graduated a finer
student. He liked archery and bowling.

The girl three houses up the road gave him
his first blow job when he was fifteen, but
he kept this a secret from his friends
because she was considered ugly and

privately, he agreed. At twenty he discovered
marijuana and smoked it often after work.

The men at his summer factory job knew this
and they all laughed about it. One day he

got high and ran over a cat. The cat belonged
to one of the factory guys' daughters, but this
was coincidence. He put the cat in a shoebox
and threw it in the marsh. As an older man his

knees sometimes shook during walks past
the spot, but he never found the shoe box
again, and thus never got to see what
a cat skeleton looked like. On the day

that he was hit by a flying golf ball, Afghanistan
crashed into New York, and many people were
too outraged to notice his eulogy on page
thirteen. Only his factory buddies

talked quietly in their bar, and all his grandparents' friends were dead, and so
were his grandparents, and so was his
alcoholic mother with big boobs.

I Am Not Your Poster Child

Yes, I am deaf. Yes, I have a gift for writing. That's not arrogance on my part. If you must know, I completely suck
at other things, such as math, baseball, and interpreting

Picasso's cubism from a Neo-Marxist standpoint. So it all balances out.

However, there are times when my writing skills are used to justify *others'* arrogance. I remember one day about eleven years ago . . . I was working as an educational assistant in an oral program. I was arguing with one of the teachers. I don't remember exactly what she said, but it went something like this:

"Blah, blah, blah, yes Chris; but you're the cream of the crop. You can speak, you can write, you can read, you can think. You're a one-in-a-thousand miracle!"

Now excuse me, but that pisses me off! Even after ten years, the memory brings up a wave of nausea, rage, and disgust from the pit of my stomach. That sorry excuse for a teacher had absolutely *no* right to say that to me, and neither does anyone else!

Do not use my gift, or my accomplishments built upon that gift, as an excuse to justify your contempt for other deaf people. And conversely don't use it to justify your benevolence toward them. Don't put me in that position. I don't want to be there, and you do not have my permission to put me there.

Let's ignore the speaking, reading, and thinking thing for now. Let's just focus on writing. As mentioned earlier, yes, I can write. I can write a damned sight better than most of the hearing people I have met in my life. But that's not the point.

I repeat; my writing is a *gift.* It was one out of a billion possible gifts that Fate happened to drop on my lap cells while they were still multiplying in my mother's womb. That's the gift I got. I didn't get most of the others that are available in the human gene pool, and I don't remember Fate ever offering me a say in the matter. I developed that gift through endless hours of honing my skills, yes. But it also developed through luck of a dozen different kinds: being able to hear a lot as a kid, a good education (both oral and manual), and chance exposure to brilliant writers as well as awful ones.

And that *is* my point: Opportunity and luck of the draw both played their parts. My gift is not just the result of some big mass thing called "oralism." Nor is it just the result of learning ASL or any other single reason.

And hey, I'm sorry if that disappoints you. Really, I am. But I am not your spokesperson. I am not evidence of your pet theory. I am not your example. And I am not your role model. You never asked me if I wanted to be these things, and I never said yes or no. So don't try to make me feel proud of having something that few people—deaf or hearing—have. Don't try to make me ashamed of it either. That's not your place. Your place is to feel how you want to feel about—and do what you want to do with—your *own* gifts. Leave me out of it.

And if all of this pops your personal Savior Bubble, well . . . I'm sorry about that too.

Corresponding Oval

I think appropriate suicide methods
are one day going to be taught
in kindergarten classrooms.

Tut, tut, children!
Yes!
How many times do we jump?
Once!
And how many times do we cut?
Once!
Which way?
Deep!

* *

Let me tell you about contempt.
When I die I'm going to fuck with
people's corresponding ovals.

I'll sugar-coat a gun barrel with cyanide honey,
put it in my mouth, and lick myself to death.
My teeth will shatter around cold blue steel
in a rigor mortis grin, but I will die happy
simply because there will be no corresponding oval.

How did he die?
  Gun ( ) Poison ( )

* *

Let me tell you about contempt.
I would bleed off balconies yet not jump,
since I can't jump off balconies and not bleed.

I would slice my wrists shallow
yet lean not-very-far over the railings.
I would specifically try to hit older women,
splatter the fake white doves

on their church-going hats with the red stains
of my life; the sports pages
of briskly walking middle-aged men
in plaid suit coats; blonde-haired
Barbie dolls of young girls attached by the hand
to Christmas-gloved mothers.

* *

Let me tell you about *not knowing.*
I think of it and smile.

When I'm dead I want my epitaph
to be a grid of Tic-Tac-Toe played over and over again
on top of itself.
Every oval crossed out by an X,
every space a question. Something filled in,
yet something not. Something uncertain,
and something uncontained. Something asleep,
yet poised—and watching.
Sometimes it watches me.

And sometimes not.

Chris, Amy, and the Floating Motion Sickness Pills

"I don't want to give up my *freedom*."

"I'm too *independent*."

"I have my own way of doing things and I *like* it that way."

"I don't want someone else coming in and disrupting my life or overshadowing my needs with their *own*."

Over and over I get these kinds of comments from my single friends. Over and over, I fail to understand them. I've been married for seven years, and I can tell you that the very thing single people seem to be the most afraid of—giving up their own way of doing things—is the best part of marriage. My wife Amy, in entirely unplanned and indirect ways, is the person who teaches me this again and again.

Example: Virginia Beach. Summer of 2004.

Now I'll tell you that, while I'm not exactly married to the female counterpart of Felix Unger (anyone remember *The Odd Couple?*), I *am* married to a woman who will not be caught dead without a plan, a map, and sometimes even a chart. Amy is the only woman I know who has the daily planner booklet in her purse cross-referenced with the calendar on our home computer. For her, half the fun of a vacation is drawing up a budget for it, marking the most expedient routes for getting to where we're going, and creating a checklist of Top Ten Sites to See.

I, on the other hand, have about as much patience for planning as a six-year-old in Toys "R" Us. During graduate school, "housework" for me meant letting used pizza boxes pile up in only the living room (the bathroom had to be kept clear for the piling up of stale towels), and "dinnertime" was a burger and fries at 10 p.m. in the nearest sports bar.

So as you can probably guess, quite a few of the early days in our marriage were scenes from *Shrek* (before Cameron Diaz turned into a female ogre). Over the years, I slowly accustomed myself to the alien concept of being home at 5 p.m. and doing dishes twice a day instead of once a month. She accustomed herself to the spontaneous and adventuresome idea of renting *two* DVDs for the weekend (and possibly even seeing a movie on top of that!) instead of renting just one a year. It was tough, but we persevered; and seven years later, our weekend minigetaways were things of mini-wonder!

Not long ago we went to Virginia Beach for some fun-n-sun. Amy drew up the map, planned the budget, and reserved the hotel room a month in advance. I met her halfway by packing the night before (instead of forty-five minutes before we left as I normally would have) so that we could leave at her usual 6 a.m. instead of my usual 3 p.m.

I was a complete zombie in the car—I think it is somewhat ungodly for the world to start itself up before 11 a.m.—but managed to catnap my way into alertness by the time we arrived at the beach three hours later. Amy was happy and skipped all the way to our hotel room, which overlooked the ocean and was really cool!

An hour later, we were hitting the sand and the surf. Virginia Beach is packed with tourists posing for Kodak Moments.

Medium-sized tidal waves catch them unawares from behind and toss them, sputtering, into shallow pools of foam with their shorts wedged up their butts. Great entertainment! Amy and I thoroughly enjoyed our day, sitting out tanning until the sun went down. Then we decided to go for a walk along the boardwalk.

During our walk, we happened upon a gift shop with an advertisement for parasailing taped to its display window. Needless to say, I was beside myself with excitement! I pointed, I pleaded; I argued that the ocean might boil away in some global warming mishap before we would ever again have such an opportunity! Only $80 for 1,200 feet! My God, who could resist?

I knew that there was probably no way Amy would ever go up, even at lower heights (the minimum height was 600 feet), but I was hoping she might. As it turned out, she wanted to but just couldn't muster up the courage to go even that high. As a compromise, however, she said she'd come out on the boat and take pictures as *I* went up.

Now this was a big thing for her, and I appreciated the gesture. Amy gets motion-sick quite easily and therefore finds planes and boats to be excruciating hell even though she's afraid of neither heights nor water. So when she said we'd need to walk to the drugstore to buy motion sickness pills, I didn't tease her about it, not even when she outlined her plan for taking one that night and one the following morning right before we were scheduled to go and meet the parasailing boat at the harbor. I was just so overjoyed at the prospect of both going up and having her there with me (or at least on the boat), it was all I could do to keep from turning cartwheels through the drugstore.

Upon purchasing the motion sickness pills, we decided to leave the boardwalk and head back to the hotel by walking along the beach instead. It was another moment of romantic spontaneity. Amy asked if I wanted to walk in the sand or along the water, and I of course chose the water. We took off our shoes and held hands and felt the cold surf wash over our feet.

You'd think I would be entirely satisfied with such a moment. But no, I had to push it one step further by telling Amy I wanted to go for a quick night dip in the water. I handed her my shirt and shoes. I didn't have my wallet or keys on me. They were back in the hotel room—no need to check my pockets.

This is why I forgot to remove the motion sickness pills we had just bought.

Ah, the moments where spontaneity and planning meet are truly amazing ones. Sometimes both break down entirely, such as the moment when a fifteen-foot wave crested over my head and tossed me like a little toy into the surf. I'm a strong swimmer—I breast-stroked right out of it without missing a beat. As I turned my face to get air, however, I noticed a little white box floating on the surface of the water and absent-mindedly cursed the pea-brained polluters who destroy our oceans. Of course by the time I came back out of the water, Amy asked me where the pills were, and I sheepishly realized the polluter was *me*.

But you know what? It didn't matter. Amy was a little bit grumpy when she went to bed that night, but we got a new box of motion sickness pills first thing the next morning. She came out on the boat! I went up 1,200 feet while she took pictures and waved at me! I will never forget looking down at the schools of dolphins playing below. I'll never forget landing on the boat and hugging Amy and screaming, "Did you see? Did you see! Wasn't it cool!?!" I will never forget her smile and laughter and the easy, light feeling we had during the entire drive back to Alexandria.

My single friends tell me they would never want to give up their own way of doing things for the sake of a relationship. I think about the floating motion sickness pills and being dripping wet while hugging my wife (because she had convinced the boat captain to slow down and dunk me in the water).

It's giving up your own way of doing things and meeting someone else halfway that can create some of the very best moments of your life. My single friends never understand what I'm talking about.

But I hope they will someday.

Five Beers Away

My grandfather was a bartender for the better part of his life. Maybe you've seen the place—Erv and Gertie's Tavern in Oak Grove, Wisconsin. After my grandparents died, the bar was sold off to someone else and renamed. I don't know what it's called now.

He always let me work behind the bar, even on weekends. An iron-wheeled wagon ran him over when he was a kid, so as an older man he was always fighting off infections in his leg and hobbling about with his walker. My job was to do all of the running around. After a person ordered, I'd get the beer bottle out of the cooler in the back and hand it to my grandfather (the whiskey he poured himself). I had other odd jobs too, such as washing the glasses and sweeping the floor. It was a great time! I was the only seven-year-old in the entire place! I even got paid—one soda and one candy bar for every night I worked for him, plus all the jukebox change I wanted!

I saw plenty go on, believe me. A decade would go by before I fully appreciated some of the things I saw, but that's okay. The education came in handy. One thing in particular that I remember: a slight difference between two questions my grandfather would ask when serving people.

When a guy first came in, Grandpa would greet him and go, "So what'll ya have?" That was my cue to get ready for a beer run. And then this guy would start drinking. Your average bottle would last anywhere between ten minutes and a half hour. All I really had to do was keep an eye out and be close by when it was almost empty.

But once a fellow had his fifth beer or shot or whatever, my grandfather would switch over to a new question. Now he'd ask, "So what's it gonna be?" That was my cue to keep getting beers if necessary but to stay away from that particular guy for the rest of the night. Because chances were *that* was the guy who was going to get obnoxious sooner or later. Rowdy, my grandfather could handle. Obnoxious, he didn't like. He had a bad leg but a strong arm, and he kept a cane behind the bar that he'd whack on the countertop if someone pissed him off. He never needed a bouncer—he could handle himself. Grandpa just wanted me out of the way if it ever came to that.

Over the years, I've thought a lot about the difference: "What'll ya have?" vs. "What's it gonna be?" The former question is one you ask to a class of people who aren't bent on destroying themselves. The latter is a question for the ones who are. The line that divided the two categories, in my grandfather's eyes, was five beers away. After that, it stopped being about choice and started being about need. He never stood in the way of either; his place in the world was to sell people booze, not make them buy it.

I like to think, though, that the two questions were his way of trying to get through to people. "What's it gonna be?" was his attempt to give them a wake-up call. Some guys at that point actually paid their tab and went home. If Grandpa saw them again, their reward was "So what'll ya have?"

It was a question he asked his friends. Everyone else was just a customer.

Christmas Is Filling Up a Dinky Little '01 Toyota Corolla Gas Tank

Ah, Christmas. Time of glowing Yule logs, time of migraines.

First, the logistics of our annual Going Home for Christmas Trip—my wife and I hail from Ladysmith and Juneau,

Wisconsin, respectively. In good weather, it takes about fifteen hours to get to Juneau, and then it's another five hours up to Ladysmith.

But keep something in mind . . . Wisconsin is as far north in this country as you can get, and in any part of Wisconsin, wintertime is not what most people would consider "good weather." Let me put it this way—I've lived in Virginia now for seven years. If a single snowflake were to drift down from the gray skies, all Virginians within a ten-mile radius would run screaming in terror. They would board up the windows of their homes and shut down the entire city of Washington, D.C., for a week.

On the other hand, Wisconsin. Do you know how the Mississippi River was formed? All the Minnesotans plowed their snow east, and all the Wisconsinites plowed their snow west. When these massive snow piles along the border melted in the summer (which lasts only from June to August. . . . Then it's winter again), the water flowed south, eventually forming what is now the Gulf of Mexico.

But getting back to my Christmas trip. . . . Perhaps you've guessed that I'm not talking about the five-hour drive between Ladysmith and Juneau. Oh, no, with 100+ pounds of presents taking up all available space in our dinky little '01 Toyota Corolla (this is before the 235-pound husband and the 120-pound wife insert themselves into said dinky vehicle), such a trip is merely difficult. And in this book, we don't concern ourselves with the "merely difficult."

Rather I am talking about the full fifteen-hour drive from Alexandria, Virginia, to my parents' house. Upon arrival, the plan is usually to stay for a day to rest and unload half the presents (translation: My wife rests, I unload the presents). After all that, only then do we make the additional five-hour drive up to Ladysmith through what *Wisconsinites* consider "good weather." That's about a twenty-hour drive, total.

We stay up there for a few days with my wife's family and then come back down to spend some more time with my family. Then we see our friends for an all-too-brief New Years Eve. By the next day, we are on the road again. I've made this Christmas trek every year, and I would have made it again *this* year with nary a negative peep . . . except my two sisters pissed me off.

Backtrack two weeks in time and clear across the country to Los Angeles, California, where one of these two sisters, Julie, lives. Julie can only get off work for three days this year: the 26th, 27th, and 28th. She calls my other sister, Heidi, and tells her this.

"Oh good!" squeals Heidi from her comfortable little country home conveniently located about eight miles from my parents' house. (You can run the distance on foot in under an hour and, ironically enough, arrive before most Wisconsinite drivers.) "We'll meet on Saturday then and have a big family get-together!"

"It will be perfect!" Julie squeals back. You've never heard voices on phones squeal so much, not even through ones with bad connections.

Two weeks later, good old Christopher gets an e-mail about all this in Alexandria, Virginia. This is known as the Annual Christmas E-mail because it's more or less the only time Christopher ever hears from half of his siblings.

"Oh no!" cries Amy, Christopher's wife. "We'll be up in Ladysmith at that time! Whatever shall we do?"

"Fear not!" Christopher's voice carries the inspiring confidence of a man with an idea. "I shall call them!"

"See if we can come down on Sunday," Amy says.

Bammo, Christopher picks up the phone and calls Los Angeles, California. Phones are funny in that way. Phones do not have to make fifteen-hour drives over entire mountain ranges in weather that most people would not consider normal (not even Wisconsinites). When I die, I want to come back as a Verizon cell phone. I will travel the world on a cheap weekend plan and never pack Christmas presents again.

On the phone, even through the relay, Julie is shouting. Wake the dead, wake the deaf, all the same to this girl. "What?!? You can't come down on Saturday?

"Well, we. . . ."

"That's only *one day* with you! I haven't seen my brother in a year and a half!"

"I know! But. . . ."

"Well *excuse me*—I'm a criminal! I want to see my brother!"

When the people you're talking to start referring to you in the third person right to your face, you know you're in trouble.

I hang up the phone and consult Amy. She is not pleased—she wants time with her family, too, and I want to avoid making multiple trips between hometowns. Perhaps you might be wondering at this point why we don't simply fly and gain all the driving time back. I ask you in return: Have you ever tried carrying two families' worth of Christmas presents onto a plane? Or cleverly had them stowed *under* the plane only to find, upon landing in Wisconsin, that your presents were mistakenly sent to Miami?

Then Heidi calls me.

Through the relay, she shouts, "What's this about you not coming home? You never come home! How can you not come home? Your nieces and nephews all want you to come home! Mom wants you to come home! Julie is only coming home for a short time, and if you don't come home then why should anyone come home, because Christmas is a time for coming home and *nobody is coming home!*"

I want to reply that *Virginia* is my home, and nobody has ever come to visit *my* home in the entire seven years I've lived here! But I cannot reply because the phone has melted in my hand. An online scan of the *Milwaukee Journal* that afternoon reveals that all the hot air in Heidi's call to me set the Wisconsin relay on fire.

Fast-forward in time to today. Another e-mail has arrived for me, a chorus of angry siblings berating me for my selfishness. Can't we (translation: I), they ask, make some adjustments in our (translation: my) traveling schedule?

Again, I consult Amy. We make adjustments, and a new plan is fixed. And so this year, I'm making the trip again, albeit with a little peep of dissatisfaction.

Christmas is a reflection of the health of family relationships. Healthy family relationships, even among siblings, cannot be maintained by warp speed three-day visits squeezed in between the act of hopping off and then back onto a Midwest Express 747. Relationships aren't a Verizon Wireless cell phone text message once a year.

Relationships are a lot more like those fifteen-hour drives in a dinky little '01 Toyota Corolla, bravely huffing and puffing its way over mountain ranges (sometimes through weather that even Wisconsinites would not consider "good"). You can't just fill up the gas tank once a year and presto, you're all set! Try to make *that* trip, and sooner or later, no matter how many squealing phone calls you make, you're going to find yourself stuck. Only now there's a howling blizzard outside, and the warmth is leaking out through a crack in the back window. Where's your 100+ pounds of presents gonna get you then?

If this question doesn't apply to *you*—great! Go and enjoy Christmas. But if it does, stop wasting precious time.

Go fill up the tank.

Responsibility Is Not a Burden

I absolutely hate how we sign RESPONSIBILITY in almost exactly the same way that we sign BURDEN. It's bad enough that Hearing America equates these two words, worse yet that we should reinforce their faulty thinking.

In my opinion, the one and only definition for responsibility should be the one you get from splitting the word in half: *response-ability*. If you separate it like this, you might understand how it's possible for a person to drown in an ocean of potential responses, because he never developed the ability to choose from among them (including the response of swimming). Conversely, you might also understand how it's possible for a person to possess a highly developed ability to respond, yet still get stuck in a situation where his options are nonexistent. Therefore he can't act, even though he has cultivated the ability to.

Let me tell you a story. About ten, maybe fifteen years ago, I unfortunately decided to go to one of those Thanksgiving dinners my Mom and aunts are always hosting. Only one other person in my immediate family can sign: my sister. Nobody else in either my immediate or extended family can. That meant I'd be sitting at a table for hours with four siblings, two parents, and about twenty other nonsigning relatives.

Now in that situation, knowing full well the communication difficulties that would inevitably arise, how could I take "responsibility" for myself (in the way that I mean it)? I wasn't going to be able to teach anyone enough ASL *before* dinner to enable them to communicate with me *during* dinner. Thus the responses I could make, from functional to dysfunctional, were:

1) Bring notepads and pencils (communication would then be possible for everyone).
2) Rely entirely on my sister's interpreting (communication would only be made possible through her).
3) Try to lipread (communication would be made possible only through me, or more precisely through the degree of my lipreading ability, which wasn't and still isn't high).
4) Sit there like a lump (communication would not be possible at all).

So what happened? I took responsibility for myself and my situation and chose Response #1. Result? I got one note all night. Cousin Cheryl wrote, "How is school?" to which I responded, "Great!" We both nodded and smiled. Then everybody abruptly downshifted to Response #4.

Okay, let's analyze this. First, I did not wallow in self-pity by starting out with the negative expectation inherent in Response #4. Nor did I use #4 as a punishment—passive-aggressive retaliation against my family for not learning ASL.

I started off with the entirely reasonable and healthy Response #1 and assumed I was loved by my family (who would presumably *want* to communicate with me).

Want to know why they didn't?

Since society has crisscrossed the wires between the distinct definitions of *response-ability* and *burden*, my family had a faulty perception of responsibility. They saw *all* possible responses that they could have made—even positive ones—to my proactive offer of notepads and pencils as something negative, a burden. Had they responded instead by writing to me, they could have had a conversation with me . . . a *reward* (believe it or not, I actually am a pretty good conversationalist).

But they didn't want any such "burden" placed upon themselves, not even for the duration of the course of a single dinner. It was my deafness, after all, and not theirs, so the burden should be on me. Or else it should be on those who were willing to share it (such as my sister through her interpreting). Thus they all ran screaming from their reward as if it were a punishment.

My sister kept looking at me throughout the whole meal, asking me through her expression if I wanted her to interpret. I shook my head *no*, somewhat out of hurt, somewhat out of anger, but mostly just out of disgust. What else can you feel for people who rob not only you, but also themselves?

I eventually outgrew my disgust, though, just as I outgrew the self-doubt and self-blame that precedes figuring out what responsibility really means. I realized that a lot of my past responses to tough situations were made in an environment where I had been taught no sense of personal empowerment. I had no access to validation, nurturing, or community support. Not a great place for developing an ability to respond.

A few years later, I realized something else: Through no fault of my own (even with my now much-better developed "ability"), I would, from time to time, have very few options to choose from. Or else I'd only have options that ranged from bad to worse.

When these moments pop up, I remember that Thanksgiving dinner long ago, and I remind myself that responsibility is simply the ability—my ability—to respond. Nothing more. The crappy options that are available for me to choose from do not define my personal worth. Neither does the choice to *not* choose from among them. Especially when I did not create them.

The only real burden lies in believing otherwise.

Full Circle

My brother Warren is about eight years older than me. We're both deaf, depending on what you mean by that. I sign; he doesn't. He has a cochlear implant (by his own choice . . . he got it at the age of forty-two). I don't have one. All of his friends and coworkers are hearing. About half my friends and colleagues are hearing, and the other half are deaf. At this stage in my life, though, all of them sign. If they don't, and more importantly, if they *won't*, I don't usually let myself get attached to them in the first place.

I don't think Warren even has any idea what Deaf culture *is*, and I've never really taken it upon myself to explain it to him. We don't talk that much. This isn't because there's bad blood between us or because he's a bad guy. He's a good guy! He's a good father, a good friend, and a hard worker. He doesn't wish pain upon people—I can tell you that much. He tries to help out where he can. You could do a lot worse than to have that said about you.

I have two memories that invariably surface whenever I think about trying to talk to him—to tell him who I am or about our community. The first disappoints me the most and makes me wary of him. The second, however, causes me to forgive him.

We used to work together as farmhands when I was a teenager. Warren had been working for that particular farm chain for about three years. They always needed extra help around harvest time. Once he started working there, it was always easy for me to get hired on and pick up some extra cash when I needed it.

To make a long story short, one day we were bailing hay. I was working on the wagon. The bales weighed maybe forty pounds. You loaded them onto the elevator, which took them up to the haymow where the other farmhands would pack them in. Warren usually worked up there. He'd keep an eye on me sometimes and make sure I was doing a good job and getting along all right.

It was thirsty work. After about a half hour, I got down to the last bale. I put it on the elevator and waited for it to be carried up to the haymow. Then I shut the elevator off so they could climb down and help me pull the wagon out of the way.

This was usually when we took a break: in between loads. So I started heading down toward the milk house to get some water. When I came back, Warren's boss Bob—you could call him the foreman, I guess—gave me a look. Nothing graphic . . . not disgust or anger or anything. He just seemed irritated.

Eventually a new load arrived. Bob and the rest of the guys started climbing up into the haymow again. Warren made as if to follow, but then Bob pointed at a bale lying under the elevator. I guess it fell off during the last load, and I didn't see it. Warren walked over, put it on the elevator, and climbed up himself. Once they were all off the elevator, I plugged it back in and began unloading the new wagon.

The hay started coming in fast from that point on, so we didn't get another break all day. By then I was pretty dusty and sunburned, not to mention scratched up. I made sure there were no more bales lying around, shut the elevator off, and went down to the milk house to clean up. I was bent over washing the dust off my neck when somebody slapped my back really hard. It *hurt*. I was snarling as I stood up, thinking maybe it was one of the younger kids who lived on the farm. But it was Warren.

"Bob was yelling at you the whole time!"

I was startled by his anger. "When?"

"During the last break! A bale fell off the elevator!"

"Jesus, okay! I'll check next time!"

Warren started to leave, but then he stuck his head back in the door and added, "You have to look back when you're walking away." He pointed at his eye and then back over his shoulder. "Make sure nobody's calling out to you."

* *

That's the first memory, the one that disappoints me. And it's stupid, isn't it? Such a small thing, the kind of memory you let go of; an incident you attribute to age. Warren was a young guy at the time, maybe twenty-four or -five. And I was an unruly teen—I admit it. It's a big brother's duty to keep the younger siblings in line, isn't it? So I can't blame the guy for wanting me to look good in front of the boss. Especially his boss.

Still. "You have to look back over your shoulder!" Ooh! A bale fell off the elevator! I apologize for my existence! Let's make sure we don't get the almighty Hearing People upset with us!

Back then I used to think Deaf people were a bit militant—especially the ones who would give me a hard time for talking or some other "hearing" thing that I wasn't supposed to do. Today, though, I can understand. Which would you pick? Some cultural pride in who and what you are, or a life spent looking backwards over your shoulder?

But it's hard, you see, to maintain that kind of resentment toward him.

* *

My second memory is of a winter afternoon when Warren had to come and pick me up from detention. I was in the third or fourth grade, I think. The detention was for fighting. To tell you the truth, I forget exactly what happened. But hey, mainstream a deaf kid in a school full of hearing kids and mix him up in the cruelty they're famous for. Which trait do *you* think they're going to pick on?

I won that fight by the way. I wish I could say it was the only one, or even the last one, but it wasn't. Not by a long shot.

Anyway, detention ended. The kid that I fought—his name was Doug—was being escorted, right along with me, out the front door by some teacher. Doug lived in town, so he started walking home right away. Warren was already waiting outside for me in that old white Mustang he used to have. I guess Dad had to work, so Mom called Warren's school and had them tell him to come and pick me up.

I never saw much of Warren, even way back then. It was a rough time for my family. My Dad was drinking a lot, and that was the year we lost our farm, I think. I was too young to understand a lot of what was going on. Warren wasn't. Dad called him "Big Boy" back then, and that's exactly what he was to my other brother and my sisters—the Man of the House. More often than not, Dad couldn't be that.

Warren would come home from school and spend all day plowing the fields in the big John Deere, and he'd be up before school doing the same thing. I don't think he ever had a girlfriend in high school. He only very rarely went out to parties with his friends. He never got drunk or high or anything like that. And he didn't talk to anyone. Least of all to me.

But that day he was there, magically materialized out of the cold gray winter sky. I was surprised, to say the least. I was more surprised when he pounded angrily on the roof of the Mustang and snapped, "Is that the kid who was bugging you?"

I muttered an uncertain "Yeah," wondering why he wanted to know.

Warren suddenly turned around and yelled, "Hey kid!"

Some distance up the school driveway, Doug turned around.

"I don't want you buggin' him anymore! You got that straight?!?"

Doug gave a little half-hearted wave of acknowledgement. I don't know if he was being a smartass about it or what; he was forty yards out, and it was hard to tell.

Nonetheless, for good measure, Warren shouted, "Yeah? Good!" Then he motioned for me to get into the car with a disgusted flick of his hand. As we roared up the driveway, he yanked on the wheel as we passed Doug . . . not much, but for the barest second it seemed like we might hit him. We didn't of course, and I don't even remember if Doug had to jump out of the way.

But if he did, it would have been poetic justice.

*   *

Today I'm thirty-six, and Warren is forty-four. With his implant, he can hear his daughter Ashley. Not perfectly—we've had some very candid discussions about this, and he says that hearing through an implant isn't the same thing as having normal hearing. Like me, he used to be able to hear quite a bit when he was younger, so I take him at his word on this. But at least when he's wearing it, Ashley can communicate with him. She can't communicate with *me*—at least not yet. Someday, I'll teach her to sign and then she will. It's kind of ironic, though . . . if she ever signs without speaking, Warren will once again be left in the dark. So it all comes full circle.

Meanwhile, many of my Deaf friends continue to express their disgust at hearing parents who implant their deaf kids; little two- and three-year-old babies. I'll nod and sign, "Yeah, it's all based on fear. They're trying to make them hearing."

But while I sign this, I'll be thinking of Warren.

Until he had a hearing daughter, he never had an implant. And what's more, he also never talked to anyone about getting one. In other words, Warren did it for *her*, his little girl. Not for himself. Not for anyone else.

So it's hard, you see, to really believe that he's the colonized scum I'm supposed to think he is, always looking over his shoulder and being Hearing America's bitch. He's there for his daughter, and he was there for me. That's the bottom line.

Then again, if Warren *had* learned to sign, then *he* could have taught his daughter ASL—and I wouldn't have to. And who knows? Maybe then my Deaf friends would have become his, also. And maybe we would have ended up talking a lot more than we have over the years.

Like I said: full circle.

One Guy vs. Seven Billion!
Can He Win? Can He?!?

Okay, let's break this down!

You're saying you don't have to learn to sign, because that's the way of the world! (Translation: the same tired old argument that this is a hearing world, not a Deaf one, and in a hearing world, people speak, not sign!) That *is* essentially the argument you're making, no? All righty! The way of the world! Fair enough. If that's the better argument, it should be able to hold up against a couple punches, right? So here goes! How many people are there on the planet right now? Seven billion? (We'll round it off!)

Okay, cool. How many of them do you know personally?

What, you don't know them all? Well then how do you know what the "way of the world" is? And hey, now . . . no. No rolling your eyes on this one. You started it, not me! I grew up outside this little dinky farming town (Juneau, Wisconsin!) with a population of about 2,000 people. It might be bigger by now (I haven't been back in a while) . . . so tell you what, we'll knock it up another grand so you'll see I'm willing to fight fair. Three thousand people, then! A tidy, bite-sized little number!

Okay. How many of *them* do you know?

(Gasp!) You don't know them! Well, Jeepers Creepers! Okay, how about *your* hometown? Population 1,000! Surely you can handle that!

No?!?

(Rubs eyes with a strained, trembling hand.) Are you trying to tell me that over the course of your entire misbegotten life, you haven't met 1,000 people (out of 7 billion)? Yet you *still* feel somehow qualified to tell me about the way of the world?

Tell you what, let's reduce "the world" to one guy you *do* know (me). I'm real—I'm not some phantom statistic. Put us alone in a room together—now let's make a deal. How about we leave everybody else on the planet out of it, since you don't know anything about them anyway, and they wouldn't come to back you up even if you were capable of giving them a call? Now we'll just make up one teeny little bite-sized rule: If you want to talk to me, you gotta sign!

So much for your argument, hey?

"I Don't Understand" vs. "You're Not Making Yourself Understood"

An interesting sociocultural phenomenon: After years of brainwashing, I am no longer capable of talking to a salesperson without apologizing.

Every time I go to get a movie, the Blockbuster guy says, "glah-kaddy-pok-spuffle-blimboff." This makes as much sense to me as it does to you. But how do I respond? "I'm sorry, I'm deaf, and I don't lipread. Would you write down what you just said?"

But why am I sorry? Or to put that more precisely, why should I be? If I type this book in the language of "glah-kaddy-pok-spuffle-blimboff," is it you who doesn't understand, or is it me who is not making myself understood? Who's it on, in other words . . . the burden of making something clear? Who has the responsibility?

Something has seeped through my defenses over the years and convinced me that it's *my* responsibility—that *I* am the lesser person, and everyone else is worth more than I am. It's my job to understand, and not their job to say something that's clear in the first place. It's my job to cower like a dog because the time of the hearing people standing in line behind me is more valuable than my own.

I try to fight it, but it's hard. You have to help me.

Let's make a pact. If I ever again say, "I'm sorry, I'm deaf," kick my ass and tell me to dump the apology. And no more of this, "I don't understand" crap either. I'm going to try "You're not making yourself understood" instead.

I will be polite. I won't make the Blockbuster guy play guessing games or make him the target of past frustrations. But from here on out, I'm responsible for my half of the communication, and he's responsible for his half. That's all I've got enough energy to do.

Sorry.

Praying for the Hell's Angel

An issue in public restroom etiquette: Okay, you're deaf. You desperately have to go to the bathroom, and you need to use the stall. But the stall door is shut.

Now see, this is bad. A stall door closes for two reasons: One, it's probably occupied by a 300-pound Hell's Angel (complete with a Viking helmet on his head—not the football kind) and logging chains wrapped around his knuckles, or two, it swung shut all by itself, and there's nobody in there.

But *which?* That's the thing. Hearing people resolve this issue with a "Hello?" and a polite little tap. What are *you* supposed to do? You don't want to get caught trying to peer through the crack along the stall door or have someone walk in on you while you're crouching down to check for feet under the partition, because that's just not cool, man.

And it's not just stalls either. A lot of those newfangled restaurants have those home-style bathrooms where you open the door and the toilet is *right there.* The doors have locks, and common sense tells you that the occupants of these bathrooms are supposed to *use* these locks . . . but sometimes they don't. Granted, sometimes locks don't work the way they're supposed to, but personally I think these people simply have a weird sense of adventure.

In any case, same dilemma. You've got to *go!* Where's a knock supposed to get you? Knocks are meant to elicit frantic shrieking: "Yo! Someone in here! Don't come in! Waitaminute! No! No!! Nooo!!"

That might help everyone else, but it's not going to help *you*, friend. So you're stuck with having to slowly push the door open, trying to see if anyone is inside while simultaneously trying to not look (in order to give anyone who might be in there as much privacy/dignity as possible).

Now *that's* what I call psychological trauma.

It can get so bad, you actually find yourself praying that a 300-pound Hell's Angel is inside. Him, you can count on to bash his fist through the two-inch-thick aluminum doorway in response to your timid rattling. Then you'll at least have some kind of visual cue letting you know to stay out.

Noise Paranoia

Deaf man (me)
constantly wonder:
what cover noise?
Toilet flush
fart disguise, will?
Bathwater run run—
now safe, lock door,
masturbate can?
Breathing decibel
what, exactly?

Wipe, finish. Know
bullet white? Push.
Hemorrhoid, ow!

KY squish,
yuck.

That, walls block?
Material depend?
Plaster? Concrete?
Difference which,
more? Middle night,
eyes white, look-look.

Pin drop, hear can?
Through all that?
(!)
Wall, plaster, brick?
Wow.

I Stopped Being Disabled and Nobody Knows

I'm a Metro Man. Riding the subway around is cheaper than buying a car, especially if you're "disabled." Why? Because you can go to any grocery store, tell the clerk you're deaf, and say you want a "Disabled" ticket. Such a ticket (it's orange, by the way) will last you about a week. It costs ten bucks: half of what it would cost you to buy "regular" tickets (they're White; once again, society thumbs its nose at Black people) that nondisabled Metro riders buy from the machines.

I used the orange disabled tickets for about four years after my wife and I moved out to Alexandria. You're supposed to go to Metro Center and fill out an application for a card that identifies you as a disabled person. Once you get the card—and only then—you're supposed to present it to whatever grocery store clerk you're buying your orange disabled ticket from. The card serves as *proof* that you're disabled.

They never ask you for your card though, especially if you're deaf. That's the delicious irony of the whole system; they're probably so wary of having to communicate with you in the first place that they don't bother to ask you for the card that proves it.

Anyway, about three years ago, I started feeling bad about the entire scam and stopped buying the orange tickets. Call it what you will—guilt over knowing that deafness isn't a disability, yet taking advantage of the cheaper services anyway. Or maybe just disgust at myself. Why does a *deaf* person deserve a cheaper Metro ticket? I can haul my own ass up the escalator; the guy who has to put up with more shit in this situation is the guy who has to wheel his chair over to the elevator. At half the Metro stops, it seems the damned things aren't working *anyway.*

None of that is my point, however. Rather, it's this: In a sense, when I made the decision to stop buying "Disabled" tickets, I also made the decision to *stop being disabled.* I decided to stop mooching off free or cheap services. I decided to stop expecting handouts and all of the other things that Able-Bodied America seems to resent me for.

But nobody *knows.*

I walk up to the same clerk I was buying orange disabled Metro tickets from three years ago, only now I'm trying to buy a pack of cigarettes or a disposable camera or something. What does she think of me? Am I still deaf in her eyes? Of course! I'm still signing!

But am I still *disabled* in her eyes? Probably. Because that's what she's been taught that deafness is—a disability. Make the argument to her, a hearing person, that deafness is actually a state of belonging to a cultural and linguistic minority, and she'll probably just give you a blank stare.

My decision eased my own conscience. Beyond that, what did it do?

a lot of bullets

if I had a bullet
for each person who said
stop feeling sorry for yourself,
I would have
a lot of bullets

enough to stampede a herd
of war elephants, make Conan
cry and drop his sword,

screaming, *no fair, no fair!*
I would laugh—bitch slap

him around a little.
show him who's boss;
write *Conan is a girl!*
across continental Africa
with spare lead.

but the Africans
would shout, *hey fuck you*
deaf boy, we're starving
here! and stomp around
in pissed-off tribal dances.

all of my writings would
disappear under their feet.
Conan would no longer be a girl.
none of the bullets
would have mattered at all.

Value beyond ASL,
Value beyond Breasts

Back when I was still an undergrad at UW-Milwaukee, I knew this girl whose major source of misery was that she was too beautiful.

She was a model—I can't remember the names of any of the magazines she appeared in, but this is because my brain had to make a choice: look at her portfolio and see the bathing suits she was wearing in the pictures, or carefully memorize the titles of the magazine covers they were on. Guess which choice my brain made!

The weird thing is that Susan didn't have a narcissistic bone in her body. She was my ex-girlfriend's roommate, and that's how I got to know her. In her dorm room, she was cool and nice and open. But when she went out clubbing with us? In a word: *yikes.* Guys would line up to buy her drinks, ask what her zodiac sign was, et cetera. She'd freeze them all with a glare so ugly, the *whoosh* of deflating male egos would blow out nearby candles.

One day, I asked her what was up with this.

"I don't want guys to want me because of how I look," she explained. "And that's why they're coming up to me in the bars . . . because of how I look."

I was a bit irritated by this explanation. She wasn't narcissistic, no, but the whole thing had a "Poor Little Rich Girl" quality to it. Not to be harsh, but if you don't like your looks, go give them to the girl who just lost hers in a fire. Now quick, list the complaints *she* has about it! That's how I felt back then. But now I see it differently.

Last week, I went ice skating with some friends. There were three little girls out on the ice trying to skate. They were so cute! All bundled up like that, they looked like a bunch of multicolored marshmallows!

My friend Jen and I were spinning around and signing to each other. The little girls must have been impressed because they kept watching us. Finally Jen waved them over. I thought they wanted to learn how to sign, but lo and behold, they wanted us to teach them how to spin! So we did! And I don't mean to brag, but twenty years from now, when you see them in the Olympics, you have us to thank for it, baby!

Anyway, later on I mentioned how this was the kind of cool learning experience I'd want from a deaf person if I were a hearing kid. Not just some deaf guy teaching me how to sign, but rather a deaf guy teaching me something completely different—like how to spin on the ice—while *using* sign language!

It was projection on my part. Deep down I just wanted to be able to say someone saw me, a deaf man, as being good for something beyond teaching sign language. Jen understood.

For those of you who still don't, let me put it this way: An image of Susan had crept back into my mind. Not the Susan in her bikini gracing the covers of countless midwestern regional magazines, but rather the Susan who just wanted guys to see her as having value beyond her breasts.

Plastic Souls

When we were kids, we played with dolls. As adults, we still play with them. Girls had the obvious Barbies. But hey, even the guys had dolls. Those little plastic World War II soldiers you tried to knock over with rocks at ten yards? They qualify. And the Spider Man action figure you swung around your head with twine (and accidentally tossed high into a tree branch where he remains to this day)? Him too. Sorry.

A weird thing: How we treat our dolls, both in childhood and as adults, more often than not parallels how we treat the living, breathing human beings in our lives.

Some people toss their dolls in a box, stick them in the garage, and never take them out again until their children are born. This is a good metaphor for how they treat their parents.

Some people put their dolls on shelves for display—collections of silent decorative figures gathering dust. This is pretty much the same way they treat their friends. In Doll World, there's the annual Spring Dusting. In People World, there's the annual Christmas card. Beyond that? Well, dusting *is* a chore. . . .

The sight of children playing with dolls scares the living hell out of me. Little girls lift little cups to tiny plastic lips. "Would you like some tea. . . .? *Why yes I would, thank you!*" The girl talks to herself. The doll never says anything. If it does, it has a preprogrammed tape or something activated by pressing a hidden button.

And isn't that just great? This will be her behavior all through junior high school and her first twenty boyfriends—press a button, get a response. It's the next seventy years of two nameless faces passing each other with a *"howareyoufine"* monotone chirp.

Yesterday my wife and I were chatting over dinner. After about five minutes, our waiter came up. "I love watching the two of you sign," he said (not signed, my wife had to interpret). "I'm taking a sign language class now! It's just so interesting!"

I tried to smile, you know? Be encouraging. But it was hard. I felt like a doll with adjustable finger joints. Seat me at a table, wind me up, and watch me spin—that's my purpose in the world. My only expression a frozen smile, my preprogrammed response a "Thank you."

All through the rest of dinner, I didn't want to talk anymore.

I didn't feel real.

Koko Want

(points) Koko want Super Meal #2.
You want what?
(points) Koko want Super Meal #2.
. . . you want. . . what?

The anthropologist is then consulted.
"Give him a paper and pen."

Are you sure?
"How should I know? The fries are on!"
Fine, fuck it. Here!

(writes) Koko want Super Meal #2.
I can't read his writing, man!
(points) Koko want Super Meal #2.
. . . I don't understand what he's saying!

Back comes the fry cook:
"Can I help you?"
(taps napkin) Koko want Super Meal #2.
"You want a cheeseburger?"
(shakes head) Koko want Super Meal #2.

"You want fries?"
(writes on new napkin) #2.
"I don't understand."
(holds up new napkin) #2.

"You want Super Meal Number Two?"
Nod of noble primate.
"Extra large drink with that?"
Nod of noble primate.

"Thank you!" Fry cooks
can always sign "thank you."
Something learned
from every cultural interaction.

Point A to Point B Should Be a Straight Line

I'm supposed to fly from Washington, D.C., to Monroe, Louisiana, for a friend's wedding. The connecting flight is in Atlanta, Georgia. In Atlanta, I disembark and find the new gate. Still forty-five minutes left. No problem.

I go up to the desk. "I'm deaf," I tell the desk girl, showing her my ticket. "I'm on the Monroe flight. If you announce anything, you have to give me a note or something, okay? Because I won't hear you."

Desk Girl smiles and writes, "Your flight starts boarding at 5 p.m." on my ticket envelope. She gives me a thumbs-up sign to indicate that she'll come and get me if anything changes. No problem.

At 5 p.m., the people waiting with me get up and form a line. I get in this line. There's a TV screen above the door leading to the plane. The TV screen lists three different flights. I catch the eye of Desk Girl and raise my eyebrows as if to ask, "This one, right?" She smiles and gives me another thumbs-up.

A different woman is checking tickets at the front of the line. I have my ticket and license ready. Desk Girl and her newly arrived colleague, Ticket Chick, mumble to each other for several seconds, looking right at me. Ticket Chick carefully compares my license photo with my face.

"Monroe, right?" I ask again. So that's three times now that I've asked, first at the desk, then in line with my eyebrows, and now here at the scanner.

Ticket Chick smiles and nods. No problem.

I get on the plane because I believe that someone—maybe even a whole group of people—has already sat down somewhere and carefully thought up a system that will get me from point A to B, deafness or no, with only a reasonable amount of effort on my part. I have more than done my job. So now it's time to relax, enjoy the flight, and trust in that system, right?

Ha.

* *

Now I'm in the air. I have a window seat . . . cool. Ah, look, a mountain range! I have a poor idea of what the geography between Atlanta, Georgia, and Monroe, Louisiana, is supposed to look like from 30,000 feet. But from what I remember of seventh-grade U.S. geography, a mountain range seems about right. The Appalachians or something. . . .

The plane is supposed to land at 6:20 p.m. At 6:30, we're still cruising steadily along above the clouds and the now-darkening (Appalachian?) mountain ranges. Curious but not really alarmed, I tap the arm of the nice lady sitting next to me—she has a shiny iron-blue beehive hairdo—and explain that I'm deaf. Did the flight attendant make an announcement about us landing late?

"She did," Beehive writes on a notepad.

I read this and breathe a sigh of relief. Okay, a minor problem somewhere. Ten-, twenty-minute delay. Happens all the time.

"We'll be landing at 7:45 p.m. instead of 7:30," Beehive finishes writing.

I almost don't see the "7." But then I do. "Whoa! You mean *six* forty-five, right?"

Beehive shakes her head *no.*

Now I'm getting nervous. What the . . . wait! Time zones! I flew out of D.C. and connected in Atlanta. Obviously that's another time zone, that's it! We're an hour ahead! But even as I ask the woman what time it is, a tiny voice in my mind reminds me that as you go west, it gets earlier, not later. And you can't get much further east than Washington, D.C.

Beehive circles the *7:45 p.m.* she just wrote.

In life, one generally must leave some given Point A and then head toward some distant Point B. Otherwise it's not really considered much of a life. But do you ever get the feeling that, despite your best efforts, you're not making headway toward Point B at all? Ever feel like you're going backwards?

"This is the flight to Monroe, Louisiana, right?" I ask.

Beehive shakes her head *no* again, and writes, "This is the flight to Buffalo, New York."

* *

You know how those little bathrooms at the ends of airplanes seem to be made entirely out of cheap plastic? Well I assure you this isn't true—that plastic is as hard as a rock. When you get on a plane expecting to be flown to Monroe, Louisiana, and then find out in mid-air that you're actually being flown to fucking Buffalo, New York, you want to break something. You think to yourself, "Ah-ha, I'll wreck one of those little bathrooms at the end of the airplane! Revenge!"

But you can't. They're very solid.

I have a revelation, standing here staring at my reflection in this metallic mini-bathroom mirror. The System is not set up to handle us. The proverbial Airline of Life is being run by the Seven Banana Brothers. It's a three-ring circus down there. Everyone is staggering around and crashing into each other, frantically climbing up ladders leaning against thin air.

So what do I do? This is my question for you. I'm relatively safe for the moment, locked here in a flying bathroom at 30,000 feet. Is it my fault? Do I deserve this? Am I a bad or unworthy person? Should I have asked if I was on the right flight a responsible and mature *four* times instead of an irresponsible and incompetent *three?* What is expected of me? How much more do I have to hold in? When do I become more than an afterthought?

I ask because I'm getting mad. And I'm getting sick of waiting. I'm tired of looking down and seeing everything rush backward in the wrong direction at a speed of 500 miles per hour. This isn't my flight, do you understand?

I want to get off.

But I Don't *Want* to Buy
a Deaf Person!

Based on the luck I've been having lately, I just *know* that someday the relay operator is going to relay the following conversation over my TDD:

Operator: Ringing 1 . . . 2 . . . (Answered) . . . (F). . . .

Speedy Cab: Speedy Cab, may I help you Q GA

Operator: (Explaining relay, please hold. . . .)

Speedy Cab: I don't want to change my phone service, thank you. GA (sounds puzzled)

Operator: No, no, this isn't a phone company. This is the Virginia Relay. . . .

Speedy Cab: We're already signed up with Verizon. I'm sorry. I'm hanging up now. . . . GA

Operator: Wait! No, no, I'm not selling anything! A deaf person is trying to contact your comp. . . .

Speedy Cab: I don't know any deaf people. And what is this 'GA' thing Q GA

Operator: (Sighs) No . . . listen . . . okay, a deaf person is using this relay to. . . .

Speedy Cab: We don't want to buy anything from any deaf people either. GA

Operator: They're not SELLING anything!

Speedy Cab: What do they want then Q GA

Operator: The deaf person who is calling me wants you to send a. . . .

Speedy Cab: Is this a joke Q GA

Operator: No, really, it's not! A deaf person is using this relay to. . . .

Speedy Cab: But I don't WANT to buy a deaf person! I've already got four kids at home! Now I have to work, and you're tying up my line. I'm hanging up now, okay Q GA

Operator: Uh. . . .

Speedy Cab: Please disengage the line, ma'am. And I'm not saying GA anymore!

Operator: I . . . uh . . . okay. This is a federal issue here, okay? Legally you cannot refuse this call. I'm required to inform you. . . .

Speedy Cab: I've already got four kids! If you're saying that you're putting up deaf children for adoption or something. . . .? Do you want them dropped off at a foster home? Because I can give you the number to my church. . . .

Operator: Uh. . . .

Speedy Cab: Maybe some other parents in the area might want to adopt, is what I'm saying. My priest might know. . . .

Operator: NO! Look! This call is about a CAB! A deaf person wants you to send a cab and is calling through me, a relay operator, to tell you where to send it!

Speedy Cab: I'm. . . . I'm not authorized to . . . you know, buy any. . . . We're not authorized to transport . . . uh, children, you know? Especially any, uh, disabled . . . for adoption agencies. (Clears throat) We're just a regular cab service. . . .

Operator: THIS ISN'T AN ADOPTION AGENCY!

Speedy Cab: (Talking in background) Uh, ma'am? I don't mean to sound unprofessional, but my supervisor is telling me to hang up. We don't do business with, uh . . . child transport of any kind. . . . Uh . . . perhaps there are some social service agencies you might wish to call. . . .

Operator: HE JUST WANTS A CAB!

Speedy Cab: I'm going to hang up now. . . . You're tying up our phone lines, and we're losing business talking to you. Good day to you. . . .

Operator: BUT HE JUST WANTS. . . .! (Person hung up. . . . Would you like to make another call?)

Fares

Deafness is an Arabic taxi driver,
catching just enough English
in the destination
to get the car moving.

Then it's drive, drive, drive
these gibberish-speaking fools
around New York all day,
as they smile and nod

or slap you with a newspaper.
Steering by that,
until they dash off at the corner
without paying

(leaving the door open),
or else shove cash at you
without counting, just so they
can finally get out of the cab.

Babes from Space!

I'll bet you any money that the gender who hates science fiction
the most is probably women. I find this weird because women,
far more than any other American minority, have gained the
biggest status boost from the genre.

The new *Battlestar Galactica* TV series is a perfect example. Any fans out there? If so, then you probably know that the
original series came out in the late 70s. The new series, which
will soon be heading into its fourth season, is cooler and has
much better special effects, but there are a few other changes
that I think we should take note of.

One: The stories in the new version, like the original, more
or less center around the fighter pilots of the Galactica. But
in the original series, all the fighter pilots were male. In the
remake, Starbuck is a woman (another change—in the new
series, "Starbuck" is her call sign. . . . Her name is Lt. Kara

Thrace. And thank God for that, too. . . . In the 70s version, "Starbuck" was the guy's *actual* name! How did he ever survive junior high school?).

Boomer is a woman too! In fact, and this is especially weird . . . in the original version, Boomer was one of the token Black men in a race of human survivors that apparently (99.9 percent anyway) consisted only of White people! In the new version, Boomer isn't only a woman, she's also a woman of Asian descent (score one for an entirely new minority!).

What do these things mean? I don't know! But I *love* the new Starbuck! She isn't even the most attractive female character on the show (Boomer is hotter by far); but she *is* nuts . . . a trait I admire in Viper pilots. She punches superior officers, takes on squadrons of Cylons by herself. . . . What more can you ask for? She's a woman who acts more like a guy than most guys do today. She's ten times the Starbuck that the Starbuck of the 70s ever was! I'm not saying that outmanning the men is the loftiest goal today's women can aspire to, but it's nice to see female characters on television who dig shooting evil galactic robots as much as their male counterparts.

Why bring all this up?

Well, it's probably a good sign that American society has finally managed to de-"male"-ize (sorry, *demasculinize* doesn't have quite the ring I'm looking for) and de-"white"-ize itself long enough to create such an awesome gender- and racially-mixed cast for the new *Battlestar Galactica*. Women have come a long way from the days of shows such as the original *Star Trek*, where their only job was to remain as scantily clad as possible, make out with Captain Kirk, and swoon on cue to bad orchestra music.

As Deaf people, what we need to do now is start working on getting into the remake of the current remake of *Battlestar Galactica* (which should happen in another thirty years if trends continue). Maybe by then, if we work as hard as the women have, we can de-"able"-ize society long enough to put Commander Adama in a wheelchair, make Starbuck a one-armed Chinese amputee (though her remaining arm will still be the quickest draw in the galaxy), and make Captain Apollo a four-foot-tall deaf Eskimo.

I mean, if you're going to drag the survivors of the human race across the galaxy in search of Earth, shouldn't that human race actually *be* the human race—in all of its diversity—and not just the good-looking White guys?

I Worship Cochlear Implants!

What's with this rumor that I'm against cochlear implants? What the hell is wrong with you people! I'm not against them! I love them! I *want* to hear again!

That will solve all my problems! Hearing people are perfect! They don't default on their mortgages or have their cars repossessed! They don't get syphilis, hemorrhoids, foot fungus, sties in the eyes, or ingrown toenails! They aren't date-raped by their boyfriends or beaten by their husbands! The (drum roll) Beautiful! Shiny! Hearing people. . .

. . . don't get gingivitis, bloody gums, halitosis, root rot, braces, or wisdom teeth! Their buttons do not pop off, their zippers do not get stuck, they are not grossly obese, and their toilets do not overflow! Their mothers don't die! Their fathers are not alcoholics! Their friends never betray them! God loves them, and only them—being hearing is an instant free pass into Heaven! Their cars are all Ferraris, and their homes are all built on hillsides overlooking the ocean (even in Wisconsin)! Their bellies are flat, the skin under their eyes does not sag, they never go bald (especially not the women), and they never fart!

They don't need makeup—they're ready to go as-is! They speak all languages fluently and fight better than those slow-motion guys in *The Matrix!* They don't get flat tires, their high heels don't snap off, they don't rack up credit card debt, and they don't get ulcers!

Their knees don't blow out! They all compete at least at the semi-pro level in tennis and golf! They file their taxes on time! Their hearing kids (adorable!) do not smoke marijuana, vomit beer, die in car accidents, shotgun people to death in public high schools, carpet bomb Iraqi day care centers, or forget to wear a condom!

It's only Deaf people, you see, who are: Wrong! Bad! Defective! Evil! Only *they* dress like sluts, mooch off Social Security, slack off on the job, impregnate their seventeen-year-old high school cheerleading mistresses, steal bicycles, and put razor blades in Halloween candy! They're the only child molesters you're gonna find on the block! Shun them, I say! Demon bastards, all! And probably contagious!

Do I support cochlear implants? Bah! What a question! I worship them naked! Is that clear enough for you simpletons? I frolic with them in vats of rich, purple grapes while drinking sweet orgy wine!

Amen!

Have Cell Phone, Am God

Situation: a guy driving down the freeway (at, say, sixty miles per hour) speaks into his cell phone to a friend ten miles away. "I heard you!" he shouts into the phone. "I'll meet you in front of McDonalds in ten minutes!"

Kind of arrogant of him, isn't it? That *I*.

A naked, unassisted, cell phone-less hearing human being's *actual* ability to hear extends to . . . what? The length of a football field? And Olympian athletes in top shape can sprint at what? Thirty miles per hour? And only *then* for short bursts, otherwise their lungs would blow up!

Translation: Without that cell phone, the *I* in "I hear you" isn't worth very much at all, now, is it? That friend waiting outside of McDonalds ten miles away can shout until he's blue in the face. *Nobody* is going to hear him if he's ten miles away.

The *I* in "I'll meet you in ten minutes" is likewise suspect. Under the power of his own two legs, the guy in the car could do ten miles in about . . . oh, maybe two hours. More likely three or four. And yet . . .

. . . a guy with a cell phone isn't disabled, but a guy with a hearing aid is. A car is fine; a wheelchair is a Retard Machine. Blindness is bad, but people say, "I was up reading at 2 a.m." without batting an eye. Really? They were reading in the dead of the night all by their little able-bodied selves? Without any assistance at all? From, say . . . *a lamp?*

I think people use terms such as *disabled* so they don't have to face just how pathetic, weak, vulnerable, and useless human bodies actually *are* . . . even fully functional ones. After all, human beings are Masters of the Planet, right? So what if wolves hear better than us? Or deer are faster than we are? Or bears stay warm better? People have *cars and cell phones!*

Well, hell, I'm convinced! No more $3,000 hearing aids for me, no sir! Not when I can get a cell phone *and* physical superiority for a measly hundred bucks! That's the best deal I ever saw!

With or without lamps!

Shark and Camel

Long ago, at the beginning of the Earth, people did not have voices. Only the animals could speak. But all of that changed because of Shark and Camel.

When the Creator made the animals, he sent each one out to explore its own domain. Monkey climbed high into the trees. Ram bounded up the steep mountainsides. Bird flew high into the clouds.

Camel, likewise, went out to explore his domain—the desert. He walked and walked for many miles over yellow dunes of sand that rolled outward for as far as he could see. As he walked, the mighty sun beat down upon his back. But Camel was not tired or thirsty. The Creator had protected him well, giving him a body that needed very little water.

After many days of walking across the unchanging landscape, something strange happened. The dunes abruptly changed their color just beyond the last rise. Instead of yellow, they were now all blue! And they were moving! But not in the way that the sand moved when blown about by the wind. These dunes rose and fell and crashed against one another in a big churning mess.

It was all very weird. But not as weird as something else Camel saw.

A short way out into that vast blue desert of rising, crashing dunes, Camel saw a big gray blob looking back at him. The blob most definitely did not look like him. Instead of a hump on its back, it had a flat, pointy triangle. There were two more of them sticking out of the thing's shiny gray sides. It used them to push itself around and under the rolling blue dunes. Camel had never seen anything like it before!

"What are *you?*" Camel asked, giving his head a disdainful little flick. He was more than a little bit nervous about the entire encounter and wanted to hide the fact. He was King of the Desert after all, and it wouldn't do to let his nervousness show. Bad for the reputation.

"I am Shark!" replied the weird gray blob. "I am the King of everything that lives in the water."

"Oh, that's *water!*" Camel shouted, delighted to have at least solved the mystery of the blue sand. But since he didn't want to appear stupid, he gave his head another disdainful flick and said, "We don't get much of that out here."

* *

Now Shark, for his part, was also a bit nervous. He had been swimming peacefully along the ocean bottom until all of a sudden he was no longer in deep water. He poked his head above the surface and saw something he had never seen before—a vast, rolling ocean of yellow waves! It was impossible to breathe up there—and it was *hot!* Much hotter than Shark could handle. In fact, he had to keep diving in and out of the cool blue water just to keep things manageable. It was either that or have a serious fainting spell. And passing out would not be good for his reputation.

To make things worse, there was something else up there besides weird yellow waves. An ugly brown *blob* was swimming around in them! Only it wasn't exactly "swimming." Instead it stood in one place on four long things that were covered in something that looked like brown seaweed. The blob didn't seem to have any fins. Instead it had a big hump on its back. And the hump was covered with even *more* of that strange brown seaweed! In fact, its entire body seemed to be covered with the stuff!

The whole thing was a bit unnerving, and that was bad. He was King of the Deep! You don't keep a title like that once it gets around that you don't have any guts!

"It's probably *good* you don't get much water up there," Shark said, giving his tail a mighty flick that sent a spray of salty ocean water directly into Camel's face. "For I have the fastest fins around! I could swim circles around you and sleep for a week before you even noticed I moved! *So there!*"

* *

It was not the words that made Camel angry so much as it was the salt water stinging his eyes. He gave his head a mighty shake and glared at Shark. "Is that what you call all that bobbing around that you're doing? Swimming?" His thick eyelids lowered slightly in contempt. "Try *walking* some time. Walking for days and days with *no water at all!* Think you can do it? You seem a little *hot* already there, you know?" And with that, he kicked a shower of sand in Shark's face.

Shark was able to dive beneath the waves and avoid most of it. But it wasn't the sand that made Shark angry so much as it was that final crack about being hot. He didn't need some big blob of brown seaweed telling him he couldn't handle something! He was King of the Deep! He deserved *respect!*

"Take a look at these *teeth*," Shark said, grinning meanly. "I bet you I could make short work out of you with *these!*"

"Bah," said Camel, puffing out a bit of air so his nostrils would flare majestically. "Who needs teeth when you've got *these?*" He re-balanced himself so he could stick out a hoof. "Are there rocks down there?" he asked, pointing at the waves.

"Sure," said Shark.

"Ever seen something that could crack one open?"

"No, but I haven't really been looking all that hard."

Camel smirked. "Well look no further, Water-Boy."

Shark growled deep in his throat. "Don't call me Water-Boy, Walrus-Butt."

"Water-Boy!"

"Walrus-Butt!"

"Got enough *ice*, Water-Boy?"

"How's the *diet* coming, Walrus-Butt?"

* *

They continued on like this for hours, bickering back and forth, each one bragging about how tough he was. They carried on for so long that eventually their voices reached up to

Heaven, where Creator sat listening. At first He followed the conversation with interest . . . but interest soon turned to exasperation, especially after it became apparent that these two idiot animals were going to argue until the sun went down.

When His patience was entirely spent, Creator sent down a crack of thunder and lightening and yelled, "Enough!"

Shark and Camel froze on the spot because a deep, bellowing voice riding down on a crack of lightening from the sky is an impressive (and bad) thing. And when that voice is followed by the sight of two enormous hands reaching down out of the clouds . . . well, that's worse.

Creator plucked them both up, Shark by his tail and Camel by his hump. "Listen to yourselves," He said, giving each animal a shake. "Fighting about who is better and who is worse, all because you're both so afraid of each other!"

He shook Camel again. "You, Camel, were made for the sand and the heat!" Then He gave Shark another wiggle. "And you, Shark, were made for the sea and for the deep! Each of you is perfect for your own domain! Why can't you accept this?"

* *

Now perhaps Creator would have let it go at that and put each animal back down again. But Camel, even though he looked very ridiculous hanging around with his hump all bunched up between Creator's thumb and forefinger, refused to look at Shark. Shark, for his part, looked more than a little bit huffy too. And it wasn't just because he was being held out of the water (and was therefore out of breath) either. He was just being *huffy*.

This pissed Creator off.

"Maybe you two need to be taught a lesson," He said. Suddenly He hurled Shark and Camel up into the clouds. "Why don't you go and have an argument about why you're both better than Bird?"

Shark and Camel soared up and up and up . . . which was kind of fun, in and of itself. But the beginning of the Earth was not exactly a time when either sharks or camels had practical experience with skydiving (they still don't—maybe they'll get around to it someday). The result was not graceful. Shark tried to flap his fins like a bird and swim through the air. Camel tried to flap his hooves. Neither strategy worked out very well. They both began to fall!

Alas Creator caught them before they could hit the ground. He then took a careful look at them both. But even though they were scared, they still refused to look at one another. They still hadn't learned their lesson.

"Maybe you both think that you're better than Monkey!" Creator said, and with that, He hurled Shark and Camel up into the branches of the tallest tree on the planet Earth. This caused immediate problems for Camel, whose hooves were not built for hanging onto things. Shark didn't do a whole lot better, since he had no arms at all, and his fins in this instance were even more useless than they had been in the air. He tried to hold on for a while by gripping a branch in his teeth, but his great weight made the branch snap instantly. Down he plunged, and Camel went right along with him, because Camel was on the porky side as well.

Creator again caught them both right before they could hit the ground. Now they seemed quite shaken and a bit more open to new lines of reasoning. Then again, ego is a tenacious thing. So, to be on the safe side, Creator shouted, "Or maybe Ram! How about him?" And with that He threw Shark and Camel toward the top of the world's highest mountain.

Up there, Camel did a little bit better than Shark . . . or at least for a short time. But his legs were long and spindly instead of short and squat (like Ram's). This made it hard for him to balance on the narrow ledges of the mountaintop. After a while, he lost his balance and began to fall. Shark didn't even get that far. He began rolling down the mountain almost instantly, turning into a huge rolling snowball before he was halfway down. Creator plucked them both back up again before either one could crash.

When He had them back in His hands, He gave each one of them a final shake. "Just in case you don't get it yet. . . ." Creator began and suddenly dropped each animal on the opposite side of the shoreline—the Camel into the deep blue sea, and the Shark into the hot sand of the yellow desert.

* *

This was, respectively, the most terrifying place either animal had ever been. More terrifying, even, than the sky or the trees or the mountains. Camel, for his part, began to sink almost immediately, because his body was not built for floating in deep blue seas. He began to sink down, down, down—past spiraling tornadoes of fish, past great coral reefs and long wispy strands of green seaweed. When his feet finally touched the bottom, however, he felt better, because it occurred to him that he could just *walk* out of the ocean. It was true that Creator had tossed him intolerably far from shore, but this was okay. If

Camel drank even a little bit of the water surrounding him, he could walk for a very long time. The idea seemed so foolproof, he opened his mouth for a drink.

Shark, for his part, landed in the sand of the desert. The heat was very bad, and the fact that he couldn't breathe—remember that he had been out of the water for a long time—bothered him a lot. However, one thing made him feel better. This was the fact that he could push himself along through the sand, after a fashion, by moving his fins. It occurred to him that he might very well swim his way out of the desert. . . . All he needed to do was apply a little energy from his mighty tail! Wasn't he the fastest fin in the ocean, after all? Let's see Creator try to scoop him up once he got under way! With that thought, Shark gave his tail a mighty flick.

Disaster struck quickly for both of them. Great torrents of water poured into Camel's mouth the second his lips parted. And instead of moving forward, Shark's mighty tail only buried him deeper in the sand, which began to rush in through his gills, choking him. Both animals began to drown.

Creator, being the consistently benevolent entity that He was, didn't let this happen, of course. Instead, He reached down with each hand to pull Shark from the sand and Camel from the water. Both were set gently back down in their proper places, Camel in his desert and Shark in his ocean. In the red glow of the fading sunset, both animals slunk away, ashamed. Creator was left alone to reflect on what had happened.

"Perhaps I made a mistake," He mused, watching the Shark and Camel depart. "I gave voices to the mighty animals who already have so many other gifts. Now they just use their voices to brag about themselves."

Just then, a trembling and naked human being stumbled into view. This was a truly pathetic animal. Human beings could not see well like Eagle; they could not keep warm in the harsh winters like Bear could. They could not track the scent of food like Cougar. Their claws were puny compared to those of Wolf and Lion—they were little more than fingers! They wouldn't last more than a moment in a serious fight. In fact, human beings could not do *anything* very well; they were so helpless!

They also smelled kind of bad. Creator saw (and smelled) all of this and felt sorry for them.

"I will give voices to human beings," He announced to all the animals on the Earth, "because they are so small and weak. With voices, they will have words for their ideas; and from these words, they will develop ways to build *things*. With *things*, they will find ways to rule all the domains of the animals! I know they will make good rulers of the Earth because their only gift is their voices."

And so Creator gave voices to human beings, believing that they would remain humble and never become proud or arrogant as Shark and Camel had been.

But Creator was wrong.

Again.

One Roll of Tape and Your Whole World Collapses

Idea: Let's stop telling hearing people they have to learn how to sign in order to understand deafness. Instead, let's tell them to tape their thumbs to their palms. A world they never questioned will collapse around them in a heartbeat.

What we'll do is offer a point system! Ten points for every hour they can go without taking the tape off. Twenty-five points for realizing why a cup *with* a handle is superior to a glass *without* one. Fifty more points for every successful bathroom trip that requires toilet paper. A hundred points for every disturbed expression received while shaking hands. And when some old woman in IHOP comments on how well they use forks? A thousand! Every kid who asks if they're allowed to drive? Another thousand! Every blank stare they get from their friends when trying to explain why the design of doorknobs is oppressive? Ten thousand points! And one million points for figuring this out: The problem is not *you*—the problem is the design of the world you live in. Rebuild that entire world and you win the game. But take the tape off, and you get nothing.

I say *screw* sign language classes! Let's enter a new era of understanding! The amount of time hearing people can keep their thumbs taped up is the *true* measure of their resolve to understand deafness.

Therefore . . . to those of you who think you'd really like to know what it's like to be deaf, I invite you now to come and test that belief. And to those of you who *know* you don't understand—hey, why stay so comfortable with your ignorance?

This is your big chance to find out!

A Bit Less Hearing, a Bit Less "hearing," But a Bit More of Both

Why keep telling hearing people they've "got to be deaf to understand?" This is a ridiculous argument for two reasons: One, it's within nobody's power to go back in time and be born deaf. And most hearing people are never going to voluntarily deafen themselves just to understand our plight better. Furthermore, they know that we're aware of this. The fact that we'd even make the argument simply tells them that we've already rejected them, because we've predicated their ability to understand upon an action that we already know they absolutely will not take.

And two, more than a few Deaf people I know use Deaf culture as an excuse to justify everything they do, even when what they do is the exact opposite of what other Deaf people are doing. "Deaf Time" is a good example of this phenomenon. On the one hand, we all know Deaf people who are actually capable of arriving at work or class on time. On the other hand, we all know the ones who waltz into the room fifteen minutes late, because hey, *that's the Deaf Way!* Now take both groups and put them to work for the same company, side by side. How long do you think their mutual understanding of (and tolerance for) each other, grounded solely in deafness, is going to last?

I think that if we want hearing people to "understand," then we have to look at the continuum we've created for ourselves and expand upon it. We have a range between the small "d" and the big "D," deaf and Deaf. Small "d" deaf people are not culturally Deaf, and big "D" Deaf people are. As things stand, that doesn't tell us much, because not all Deaf people agree on what it means to be culturally Deaf, and not all deaf people agree on what it means to *not* be culturally Deaf!

If that sounds confusing, good! It's our confusion that drives us, in moments of doubt, back toward the middle of the continuum, between deaf and Deaf. To go any further, in either direction, we'd have to close our minds to any new data, any new input, and cling stubbornly (desperately?) to our beliefs. If that's the alternative, who is to say the middle is not exactly where we should be?

Assume for a second that the same thing applies to hearing people, that they are also moving back and forth along a similar continuum. Only their continuum lies between the states of being hearing (small "h") and Hearing (big "H").

Now, instead of basing these labels on the degree to which they embrace Deaf culture, let's base them on their degree of ignorance and arrogance, respectively.

First, let's clear something up. *Ignorant* is not the same thing as *stupid.* Everyone is ignorant on some subjects. I know a lot about English. . . . I know much less about nuclear physics (and so, probably, do you). There's nothing wrong with being ignorant, so long as you retain a willingness to open your mind and learn once you encounter a subject you don't know anything about.

Arrogant, on the other hand, is every bit as nasty a term as it sounds. An arrogant person displays a sense of overbearing self-importance which arises from an assumption of superiority over others. An arrogant person isn't open-minded to anything. His mind is made up, and he doesn't need very much information to accomplish this. He's right, and you're wrong, no matter what, and the solution to every problem, in his view, is simple: *You* must become more like *him.* You must adopt his viewpoint as your own. He honestly can't understand your resistance to this. Why wouldn't you want to elevate yourself to his level?

That being said, let's say we define a hearing person (small "h") as a person who: (1) can hear, (2) knows nothing about the subject of deafness, and (3) cheerfully admits to this. He has no preconceived notions to overcome regarding what deaf people can and cannot do. He is completely open to different types of input. He has formed no broad-reaching stereotypes based on the last deaf (or Deaf) person he met. At least not yet. From this type of person, one should completely expect, and not become angry over, questions such as "Can deaf people drive?" or "Can deaf people dance?" He doesn't know any better, so he asks. There's no crime in this whatsoever.

A Hearing person, on the other hand, *has* formed opinions regarding what deafness/Deafness is all about. He has taken up a political position. In this sense, a raging Hearing Oralist is just as "Hearing" as a Hearing practitioner of American Sign Language. The political position itself has no impact at all on

Hearing status. What's important is the amount of fervor, the raw passion that goes *into* that position, that political viewpoint. The closer one moves toward passion, toward absolute conviction, the further away one moves from reason.

Then again, it's also not a good idea to remain completely ignorant, because reason depends on knowledge, and knowledge cannot be gained if one refuses to learn.

What hearing/Hearing people need to do is explore their continuum (which isn't bad advice for us, either). The hearing person needs to gather more information, draw conclusions based on that information, and hold onto his conclusions long enough to test them (which should be done as often as possible). This will automatically take him forward a couple of steps.

The Hearing person, conversely, needs to back away, at least a bit, from the political positions he has taken. He needs to start asking questions again, to throw his beliefs back into the mix and see what survives. In other words, both sides need to explore the middle ground. They need to become comfortable traversing its expanse, to learn to recognize its features and dimensions.

Unlike needing to "be deaf to understand," this is something both hearing and Hearing people can actually *do*. And if they do it earnestly, they may just find that the results of their self-explorations are as disturbing and unsettling as the thought of deliberately deafening themselves. They may find that, between their ignorance and their arrogance, there was quite a bit they weren't hearing all along.

And then it will be up to them to *listen*.

Minority = Pathology?

Saying that deafness is a pathological condition is simply a few synonyms away from saying that deafness is a medical condition. That, in turn, is only a few synonyms away from saying deafness is a *biological* condition.

Yet every physical characteristic of everything alive is derived from a biological condition. Both profound deafness and the ability to hear—extreme opposite states—are biological conditions. Being Black is a biological condition. So is being a woman.

Therefore the term "pathological" is actually a *negative social value.*

But guess what? From society's point of view (yes, still!), the word "Black" carries a negative social value. And so does the word "woman!"

Funny . . . how we'll hiss and frown at calling a Black man "boy" or a woman "bitch," but we'll ship a deaf child off to the hospital for his cochlear implant without batting an eye.

The Real World—Bigger than You Think

Regardless of what Hearing America would have you believe, the "English-speaking world" (as opposed to the ASL-fluent one) is not the "real" world. There are around 190 nations on this planet. Only 45 of them, or about one-fourth, list English as their official language.

The "hearing world" (as opposed to the Deaf one) is also not the "real" world. That statement is just an example of arrogance. I'd prove it to you, but you know what? Go eat a chocolate ice cream cone and a get a really bad case of brain freeze. Kiss your husband or wife on some random morning and realize just how helplessly in love you actually are. Hold your newborn son in your hands for the first time. Now tell me—were those experiences "real?"

Surprise, you just proved it to *me.*

Hangman

Since birth, one masked doctor
after another clutching
at your ankles, holding you
upside down. In a breeze
of fluttering eyelids, groups of
trembling medical students
look up to you, gathered
around your head in a huddle.

How did you go deaf?
Be a role model.
How did you learn to talk?
You can see the backs of their teeth.
Can you drive a car?

Another office Christmas party,
still with no clothes on.
Each squeeze during handshakes
barely controlled (pull yourself upright,
poke out the doctor's eyes!),
each smile suppressing the urge
to spit when spanked. One bad slap
breaks the spine. Tiny arms
go limp—another example.
Only the ones judged fit survive.

Cash My Check, You Flying Brick-Headed Rat-Pole Witch!

Whenever I use profanity, it's always a surprise to me. I blame that (my surprise, not my use of profanity) on the network censors and their creative ways of recaptioning verbal expletives into something the Moral Majority of America (cough) can digest.

Network censors seem to be taking advantage of the very lipreading fallacies that author Henry Kissor discussed in his book *What's That Pig Outdoors?* (Do you notice how that looks exactly the same on the lips as "What's that big loud noise?"). "F-ck you," for example, seems to have now become "Forget you!" in the captions. "Suck my d-ck" has become "Cash my check." "You f—ing b-tch" got downgraded to "You flying witch!"

"D—head" is now "brick-head." "Kiss my a—" has been turned into "Sniff my gas" (ironically only slightly less repulsive, when you think about it). "A—hole" once came out as "rat-pole." I even saw an episode of some cop show where "sh-t" got translated into "drat!" Now personally, I found that one quite realistic—a New York City cop taking heavy gunfire from a bunch of hoodlums in a drug bust gone bad, crouching behind the burned-out husk of his cruiser, frantically reloading his gun and yelling, "Drat!" Yep, as dialogue, that works.

None of this is my real point, however.

If you're ever tempted to criticize me for the profanity I use in my writing, I challenge you to answer the following question: Where the hell did I learn it? (See I just did it!) Certainly not from television . . . not with captioning censorship as crafty as this. Heard it around town? Please . . . I'm deaf, duh! Reading materials? Everyone knows deaf people can't read worth a *whit* (cough). From the signing of other deaf people? Gasp! You mean the innocent, child-like, not-ready-to-function-in-the-hearing-world deaf people? Please! I don't think we're mentally or emotionally capable of producing such filth, if you want my personal opinion. Not as tried and true products of the efficient and benevolent educational techniques of our hearing benefactors, no sir!

Wow, I guess. . . . I guess it must be emotional disturbance on my part! Yeah, that's it! Captioning censorship never had anything to do with it! It was my incomprehensible psychopathology that twisted what was originally "You're so plastered!" into "You're such a bastard!" I get it now! Profanity was developed entirely in my own diseased mind! This is why I need hearing people's help! I need to be turned away from Satan! I need to be cured!

In fact, I no longer even believe that censorship is real! The cops *really are* saying, "Drat!" The abusive boyfriend in *Thelma and Louise* really *was* saying, "Cash my check, witch!"

Because that makes so much more *sense!*

I am *wrong, wrong, wrong* to be using such disgusting language when *nobody else* is (not in TV world and not in Hearing America!). I repent!

I am a gosh-slammed *sinner!*

What Criteria for "Well-Meaning?"

I'm sick of seeing this phrase in Deaf literature: ". . . well-meaning hearing people."

Cochlear implants are advocated for by well-meaning but ignorant hearing audiologists. The actual surgery is done by well-meaning hearing surgeons. The children are then educated in oral schools by well-meaning but destructive hearing teachers, who, in turn, are backed up by well-meaning but whatever (pick an adjective) hearing speech therapists, psychologists, administrators, etc.

Can I just ask somebody real quick—what's your proof? That they're *well-meaning?*

It's an important question, because quite a few Deaf people I know might stop sounding so "anti-hearing" if we could all (and by default, yet!) stop assigning hearing people the automatic status of sainthood. Because they're *not* saints, at least as an overall group they're not; and if you want *my* proof, let's go to any prison. Give me a key, and I'll lock you in for the night with one of those very hearing inmates you think are so well-meaning.

Or (gasp!) are you trying to say that it isn't a sense of hearing *alone* that makes a person well-meaning? Okay then, instead of making hearing the sole criteria for being well-meaning, let's focus on the nouns. By your logic, if we scrap the adjective "hearing," then all audiologists, surgeons, teachers, speech therapists, psychologists, and administrators are well-meaning *solely by virtue of being* audiologists, surgeons, teachers, speech therapists, psychologists, and administrators . . . right?

No?

Well, I'm glad you caught that one! Because in the very same prison I intended to lock you into tonight, I'm quite sure you would've found at least one surgeon who cut up a patient while loaded on morphine. Or maybe a teacher who molested a few students. In fact, you pick a job, white collar or blue, and I'll show you a hearing person doing fifteen to twenty years.

I don't hate hearing people. Nor do I feel the need to label them "well-meaning," as if doing so will somehow *prove* I don't hate them.

Maybe we could just go back to the tried-and-true method of judging people based on their actions rather than on the group they're born into . . . or the profession they choose?

Popping the Normal Pill

You know you're being judged.
Corky squints his Syndrome eyes—
it's Big Brother of a Lesser God.
One Sesame Street Linda after another
frowns at your collection

of Marlee Matlin fantasies.
Are you using your hands appropriately?
Cooperate.
Insert yourself gracefully
into those closer parking spaces.

But the search for Braille smut
is long and elusive. Can it be found
in public libraries? What section?
How does one phrase this discreetly
to front-desk septuagenarians?
Can you disguise yourself
in disco medallions, big sunglasses,
bright orange sweatbands, and still keep
your job as a role model? Can you say,
Sure, all deaf people dress this way!
Or would that be bad?

Oh, and the Normal Pill? You know the one.
Take it, and you're no longer blind,
crippled, pockmarked with old zits.
Can you just pop one
and be done with it? Without
turning traitor, or feeling sorry for yourself?
Rebel in the other direction?

Stuck

I dreamt that I wanted
to go home.

I lived in the middle
of town, but the cabs
only took you
to the trains,

and the trains only ran
from one side of town
to the other.

I couldn't get home.

Empathy Is Not Pity

Quite a few times in life, I've had people say, "Quit feeling
sorry for yourself!" or "You're so full of self-pity!" Usually the
people who said this with the most force were, at the time,
people I considered to be close friends.

I'll tell you something; that's a disturbing thing to have happen to you. On the one hand, you're wondering—what if it's

true? Am I crossing a line here? Being too helpless? Am I draining this person too much?

But on the other hand, your reality is what it is, and somehow you have to make your way through it. Sometimes you can become so lost, you'll never find your way out of your problems unless you can safely express your feelings and thoughts. Especially to those you love and trust the most.

Now you can argue that people can pull themselves out of almost anything without help if only they try. And I agree. People can get through being fired, a divorce, the death of a parent; whatever. Boo-hoo. They cry a river, build a bridge, and get over it, sure.

The catch, however, is that recovery, if it's honest, happens in pretty much that exact order: *First* you cry, then you build your bridge, and *then* you get over it. Anything else is a textbook example of putting the cart before the horse. Bellowing at people to *drop the self-pity routine* can have the effect of freezing their recovery in its tracks. Because if a person isn't allowed to cry around you, what river will he have to build his bridge over?

In one of my counseling classes, my professor once showed us the highlights of a counseling videotape. On it was six months worth of sessions with a woman who had Battered Wives Syndrome. That is to say, the first ten sessions took place with her in a hospital bed. The next ten showed her *insisting* (yes, really!) that she was a bad person and deserved what she got. The last nine showed flickers of doubt playing across her face.

I would like to describe that face. During the first week of counseling, her right eye looked like a swollen, rotten grapefruit ready to burst open. Her nose was splinted, and most of her upper teeth were gone. This was once a beautiful woman, I'd like to add.

On her thirtieth session, the counselor finally got through. The woman realized (in however small a way) that she wasn't bad, didn't deserve what she was getting, and was, in fact, living in a deadly situation that she now had to somehow find a way out of.

Her natural reaction? She broke down and sobbed.

Now pay attention, this is important: If I had been that counselor, and you had been in that room with us, and you had seen her tears and chosen that exact moment to tell her to stop feeling sorry for herself . . .

. . . I would have tossed you out on your ass.

Grief, confusion, anger, and fear are natural emotions. Yes, there are times when people abusively wallow in them in order to get attention. Maybe the goal is to receive unhealthy caretaking from others. Who knows? Each situation is different.

But there are also times when feeling these emotions and expressing them is a step forward. At those times, "Stop feeling sorry for yourself" is a statement that makes it sound like you blame them for even *having* negative feelings!

Perhaps being exposed to these emotions is uncomfortable for you? Okay, fair enough.

Just remember something—your discomfort is your own issue and not theirs. You have the right to set boundaries. You do not have the right, however, to punish other people for your discomfort or to shame them for feeling bad about bad things. That's not empowerment. That's emotional abuse.

And while you're chewing on that one, here's something else to think about: If you keep throwing out "Stop feeling sorry for yourself" without thinking about what you're doing, without fully understanding the trauma involved, without understanding the effects that trauma has on the mind, and without understanding (or caring, it seems) how vulnerable a person is at that particular time . . . you can screw up someone's recovery for years. And possibly for life.

Pity and empathy are two different things. Learn the difference.

Reborn, Karma-Style

Karmic justice: Hearing people who spend their lives deliberately oppressing deaf people are born deaf in their next life. I spend so much of every Deaf education workday in such a surreal fog of déjà vu—I'm pretty sure that this is, in fact, exactly what happened to *me*.

That leads me to another thought on this subject: Deaf people who live out their lives in apathy are actually living under the delusion that they were reborn into this life as deaf *people*.

In actuality, they were reborn into this life as leeches.

He May Not Understand, but He Still Ranks a Five

Ladies? Tell you what—I'll be brave and flat out admit that I, as a man, will never understand what it's like to give birth.

Okay? You win. All of your helpful analogies have convinced me ("To understand childbirth, swallow a gallon of water, hold it for nine months, then lay on your back and try to pee with your feet set in stirrups."). There isn't one more episode of *Oprah* I can watch that will help. For all men everywhere, I surrender.

But let me ask you something: Is a man's "understanding" really the most important thing?

Are you actually gonna have a deep heart-to-heart with your husband about the *Roles of Women in Society and the Impact of Child-Rearing Upon Male-Dominated Corporate America* when labor kicks in? Or is it enough, at that precise moment in time, that he merely be capable of driving you to the friggin' Emergency Room?

While it's true that men are never going to "understand" childbirth, think on it: When it comes to guiding you through this ordeal, on a scale of one to five (five being high), what score would you give a male gynecologist? As opposed to guys like myself—puny little English teachers who can walk you through a first- to third-person grammar conversion but who, in a rush of panic, might not be able to tell you the difference between orthopedics and an orthodontist?

I bring the whole thing up because a lot of deaf people have a similar problem. They have their doubts that they'll ever make hearing people "understand" what it's like to be deaf.

Okay, let's accept that as true. The question now becomes . . . can we all move past it?

I argue that there's a difference between being able to *understand* something and being able to *do* something. A pilot can fly a plane without understanding the components of its engine or the physics of aerodynamics. It'd be nice if he knew a little something about these subjects as well, true. But in a pinch, I, for one, would be perfectly satisfied if he simply knew how to *land*.

And no, that's not a standing excuse for borderline incompetence. But there's a lot to be said for people who, although they may not understand, learn to do their jobs well enough to get them done. There's always the type who isn't willing to do even that.

In fact, there's an emotional ranking system for judging people like this. Take men who will never "understand" childbirth. On the bottom, you've got the ones who vanish (along with next month's rent money) an hour after you tell him you're pregnant. At the top, you've got the guy who steals your copy of *What to Expect When You're Expecting* and reads it while you're asleep, rubs your lips with ice chips between contractions, and lets you break his fingers during the Final Push, because letting go of your hand while you're giving birth—his respect for Women's Liberation aside—is not something that occurs to him just then.

Hearing people are the same way. They'll never understand what it's like to be deaf—you're absolutely right about that. They

can't, because they aren't deaf. At best, all they can do is speculate, just like all I can do is speculate about how badly it must
hurt to actually give birth (I'm guessing . . . pretty badly).

Should deaf people hate them for that? Uniformly and with
no distinction whatsoever? Or is that maybe just a tad . . .
unreasonable? I don't know, but if a hearing person is willing
to meet me halfway, I'll meet him halfway. And in doing so, between us, we have a much better shot at reaching some kind of
mutual understanding than you do . . . snarling and glowering
way over there in the corner, demanding the impossible before
you'll take even a few steps forward.

Why Must We Know?

Every semester, my students at Gallaudet ask me: "Are you
hearing or deaf?" For weeks prior to this question, they'll watch
me. They see me in my office talking on the phone—*he's hearing!* Then they see it's Voice Carry Over—*no wait, he's hard of
hearing!* They'll test this theory in a variety of ways. They'll
yell behind me in class when I'm writing on the chalkboard. I
don't respond—*he's deaf!* They'll slam the door too hard and I
jump—*no, he's hearing!* But then someone will helpfully point
out that maybe I just felt the vibrations.

Damn!

I escalate their turmoil by playing little mind games with
them. They ask me again if I'm hearing or Deaf.

"I'm Chris," I respond and look at them blankly. Newborn
fawns could not appear more innocent. Obviously I have no

deeper understanding of what they're asking me, no recognition at all of the cultural overtones—*he must be hearing!* About a week later, I'll casually mention that I received my first pair of hearing aids in the first grade. *Damn, is he hard of hearing!* They'll probe a bit and ask if I like music. I tell them I can't hear music—*he's deaf!* But in the next class, we'll analyze the lyrics of a Billy Joel song. At the end of the lesson, I'll wink and dance a little jig, humming to myself the whole time.

It drives them nuts, I swear to God. Eventually their patience wears thin, and the issue starts to disrupt the class. They'll begin to debate my identity more and more openly. Every semester this happens, until one day I turn and write the following question on the chalkboard:

"Why must we know?"

Sometimes I underline the word *know*. Sometimes I underline *why*. Nobody ever answers the question.

Red Is Stop, Deaf Is. . .?

You must stop at a red light or you might kill somebody. You do not, however, have to stop for an apple, which is also red. The point? We can't say it's the *red* in the stoplight that makes us stop—otherwise we would never be able to drive by an apple orchard.

What makes us stop is the meaning we attach to the thing. That meaning is developed over the course of a lifetime, from preschool to Driver's Ed. If we color a stop sign green, our kindergarten teacher growls at us. If we run a stoplight in Driver's Ed, the cop (he *looks* like a cop, anyway) sitting next to us during the road test growls even louder.

Which is good. I'm not arguing against the merits of stopping at red lights. I am trying to say, however, that the color itself has no inherent meaning. *Stop* could just as easily be royal purple or cornflower blue. If somebody starts training us early enough to stop at pink fuzzy rectangles, that's what we'll do.

Labels are the same way. I say "Black." What meaning do you attach to the word? Do you see some hooded drug pusher in a DC alleyway? I say "woman." What do you see? A housewife? Tits and ass? Don't lie.

I say "Deaf."

What do you see? Do *all* Deaf people have to sign in ASL? Do they all have to dislike cochlear implants? Can they want hearing babies and not Deaf ones?

Is there enough room in your mind for everything deafness can be? Or do you have to chop the arms and legs off of deafness so it fits into some cookie-cutter image you can live with?

Tell me what deafness means to you. And tell me . . . who was growling at you while you made up your mind?

That's You, That's Your Beer—
Keep Them Separate

I see this again and again: A mother confides in me that her mainstreamed Deaf child has low self-esteem because he doesn't have any friends. My Deaf friend tells me her self-esteem is currently low because her boyfriend just broke up with her. A Deaf student blames his shattered self-esteem on the "F" I just gave him on his paper.

These types of statements puzzle me. What do friends have to do with a deaf child's self-esteem? What does your ex-boyfriend have to do with your self-esteem? And an "F"? What does that have to do with. . .?

I think somebody is getting the terminology mixed up, here. We're not talking about *self*-esteem. . . . We're talking about *other*-esteem. They're not the same thing. The two concepts share an overlapping influence, yes, but there's a point at which they separate.

A quick illustration of what I mean: Put your right hand over your heart and your left hand on your beer. Your heart, that's you. Your beer? That's your beer. You, Other. Get it? If you look for self-esteem in your beer, you'll feel pretty damn good so long as you actually have beer. But there's a catch. . . . When your beer is gone, your self-esteem will be too. There are many people who don't understand this. They're called alcoholics.

I find it weird . . . how we'll see these selfsame alcoholics, drug addicts, sex addicts, whatever . . . and think, "My gosh, those people must have such low self-esteem." And hey, two points for us; we're right!

But then we go home to our wife who *makes us happy.* We get a promotion and tell our friends *so they will be proud of us.* We don't marry the girl we love *so Mother won't drop dead of a heart attack.* And all the while, we remain cheerfully blind to the fact that we're a stone's throw away from being alcoholics. It's just that instead of beer, we're drinking up the approval of our wives, friends, and mothers with iffy hearts.

We cross the line when we live our lives entirely for others and never for ourselves.

To the mother of that deaf child: Teach your kid self-esteem so it doesn't go away when his friends do. And to my Deaf friend whose boyfriend broke up with her? If you're going to go looking for self-esteem in your relationships, you'll probably have better luck if you start up one with yourself.

And to my student whose self-esteem took a nosedive because he got an "F"? Quick experiment: Put your right hand over your heart, and with your left hand, hold out your failing paper. Your heart, that's you. Your paper? That's your paper.

You, Other. Get it?

Guess What? My Hearing Ancestors Had Sex Too!

I never know how I'm supposed to react when a DoD (Deaf of Deaf) tells me he's "third-generation Deaf" (or fourth-, or fifth-. . . . The higher you go, the more prestige his family is supposed to have).

Look, don't get me wrong. If you're proud of your family and your heritage, that's great. If your great Deaf grandmother out-drank Wyatt Earp and convinced him to fund the Dodge City Signing Saloon, good for her. And that's a story I don't want you to skip.

But understand something. You telling me that you're fifth-generation Deaf means exactly as much to me as the statement "I'm a fourth-generation German" means to you (I'm not. . . . It's just an example).

Do *you* care? Didn't think so.

When all is said and done, the fact that you're fifth-genera-tion Deaf means exactly one thing: Your Deaf ancestors from five generations ago had sex and produced their second (your fourth) generation of Deaf ancestors, who in turn had sex (hope-fully with somebody *else's* ancestors) to produce the third. . . and so on.

That's what you're bragging about: the fact that your paternal and maternal grandparents had sex (as individual couples. . . . Let's not make this too kinky) so your mother and your father could eventually get together and have yet more sex. Is it any surprise that I look a bit uncomfortable to you? You tell me you're fifth-generation Deaf, and I basically have to visualize your whole friggin' family getting it on.

Eh. It's okay, I guess. Maybe I'm just envious—so far as I know, I have nothing at all in common with my ancestors . . . to the point where I sometimes find it difficult to believe I'm even related to my own immediate family (I'm sure that at times they feel the same way).

But please don't get all *snotty* about your lineage, okay? More than a few Deaf people I know look down on me because my parents are hearing. I respectfully remind you that—hearing or no—they had sex just like *your* parents did.

But between the two of us, *I'm* not the one trumpeting the fact to the whole world every time I introduce myself to somebody.

Deaf Rumor Mills—The Surest Path to Absolute Freedom

You people have got to stop trying to avoid the Deaf rumor mill. You're not going to escape it no matter what you do. So why not make it work for you?

I personally make it a point to start up one new rumor about myself every week. There's a fine art to these things. Unmitigated bullshit, surprisingly enough, nobody will believe.

So if you heap on too much too fast—for example, if you start impregnating a new college freshman every day—people can't shake their skepticism, and the whole thing ends up getting treated as a joke.

What you've got to do is create a hypnotic aurora in which people can be coaxed into unconsciously suspending their disbelief. You can practice this by making yourself gay.

It really doesn't take that much work, even if you've been solidly and happily married to your wife for over seven years. Start by simply bringing up (in class if possible, but casual conversation works just as well) the fact that you've seen the movie *Kinsey*. Subtly place yourself at a "two" on the homosexuality-heterosexuality continuum. This is okay, trust me. . . . Kinsey himself implied that many people occupy this slot even though they'll ferociously repress any conscious awareness of the fact. Finish up by having an extra glass of wine at the next art gallery you attend and launch into a brief but earnest narration on the history of shading techniques used in the depiction of male nudity. You'll be gay before the weekend is out.

Similarly, it's relatively easy to acquire a budding drug problem simply by bringing a bottle of Tylenol to work. If you really do have a headache, pop a couple during your next department meeting or, better yet, pretend to swallow directly from an empty bottle. Without making it obvious that you're trying to be discreet (dizzying, isn't it?), wait for someone to notice you and then hurriedly stuff the bottle back into your pocket. Offer up an embarrassed grin and sign, "I'm addicted to these things." Then pay intense attention to whoever is holding the floor until the meeting is over. Within a week, you'll be a crack addict.

The thing you can have the most fun with, however, is getting fired. I cannot emphasize this enough: Every chance you get, get fired. For the most outlandish reasons possible. Teach class naked. Tip peoples' wheelchairs over. Crumble in front of the Dean and confess that ever since you found Jesus, you don't like his daughter anymore. This is the kind of thing people can't get enough of. If somebody stops you in the hallway and asks you why you're still hanging around ("Weren't you fired last week?"), simply shrug and say the decision was overturned on appeal. You'll be a legend within the month.

Why would you want to do something like this?

Simple: True strategic thinking is not about following a fixed plan, with the goal of arriving at Point A in order to execute Action B. No, no. . . . A strategically viable position is one that offers you the most options. The more options you have, the greater your advantage is over your opponent. Therefore, if you start up one new rumor about yourself every week, what will eventually happen is: (1) people won't be surprised by anything you do, and (2) people will have heard so much crap about you by now, they won't believe the rumors even when you're nailed for something you actually *did* do.

Which leaves you that much freer to do whatever you *want*.

Backstabbers Aim for Your Back, so Why Cover Your Ass?

People complain that backstabbers in our community are so brutally efficient at what they do because nobody ever sees them coming. Well, take that reasoning one step further. Why don't you see them coming? Could it be because you're too wrapped up in being extra careful? (Translation: covering your ass?)

You see, in a fight, there's nothing of strategic value in your ass. It's mostly just fat, even if you have Buns of Steel. It can take quite a few kicks (even good swift ones!) and be none the worse for wear. So why waste time defending it?

Ah, but your back. Now *that,* you need. It protects your spine. Without your spine, you can't stand, neither literally nor metaphorically.

Thus I offer you the following advice for countering a backstabber: First, turn around! It's difficult to get stabbed in the back when all you're offering as a target is your front.

This move, however, makes your heart vulnerable to the blade (again in both the literal and metaphorical sense). So second: Get your hands off your ass. If you stop using them to protect what isn't important anyway, you'll find that they can be of enormous use in blocking things. And while we're on that topic, it also might actually help to keep your eyes on the backstabber, because you can't block what you can't see.

And now for a final piece of advice:

If you're squeamish about the idea of defending yourself efficiently, remember something. You weren't the one doing the stabbing. You didn't start this. So dump the guilt and screw the fear. As bad as these things might make you feel, trust me, a knife handle sticking out from between your shoulder blades will feel worse.

I Am a Crab

One of my students was presenting on Crab Theory in class. For the ignorant among you, I'll let my student tell you what it's all about.

She signed (I'm paraphrasing): "Crab Theory is an analogy that refers to the destructive practice of Deaf people pulling down, by putting down, successful Deaf persons. Examples of how they might go about doing this include gossiping and spreading rumors, either in person or via e-mail. The analogy is based on the real-life behavior of crabs. Imagine that several crabs are captured and tossed into a bucket. One crab tries to escape by crawling up to the rim, but the other crabs pull it back down. The act is most likely an instinctive startle response on their part. The result is that no crabs ever escape the bucket. In human beings, the equivalent behavior is attributed to selfishness rather than instinct, although the startle response theory still applies." *

---

*For what it's worth, this was the Internet address my student was talking about: http://www.rainbowwriting.com/index4a.htm.

"Okay, cool," I said. "Who came up with the term?"

"Matthew S. Moore, the editor of *Deaf Life*."

"He did?"

"Yep, it says so right here." She held up something she had printed off the Internet.

"Are you sure?"

"Of course."

"I don't doubt you. . . . I'm just saying, I've read that before. It was . . . uhm . . . Dubois, I think. Yeah. W. E. B. Dubois. If he's not the originator of the term, he certainly got around to writing about the general idea a lot sooner than anyone in *Deaf Life* ever did."

"That's not true!"

"Sorry, but I think it is. In fact, I think something like that shows up in the book *The Souls of Black Folk*."

"You lie!"

"No, really! Dubois was referring to internalized oppression and its effects. . . ."

"You're putting down Matthew S. Moore!"

"I'm. . . . Hmmm ?"

"You're engaging in Crab Theory right now!"

"I am?"

"Yeah! You're jealous of him! He's the editor of *Deaf Life*, and you're just an English instructor!"

"I've never even met the guy!"

"Since when is the act of backstabbing dependent upon meeting your victim?"

"Look," I growled, "Dubois wrote *The Souls of Black Folk* way back when my grandfather was a kid. Between 1900 and 1910, for sure."

"I think it's just pure envy on your part. You can't stand seeing a Deaf person more successful than you are, so you rip him in half without ever having met him!"

"Uh. . . ."

"You should be ashamed of yourself!"

"I can bring in the book. . .! Show you!"

"Screw this! I can't take an English class under an Audist Crab!"

Who Says Oralism Failed?

Who says the oralism movement failed? If its primary drive is to get Deaf people to talk, I'd say it has succeeded admirably already! Because that's all most of them do: talk, talk, talk!

They go to NAD conventions, and they talk! Enrollment at their institutions is circling the drain, and they talk! Their graduates are still reading at a fourth-grade level . . . and they talk! They're still pretty much ignored by Hearing America, and to counter this they. . . .? You guessed it! Talk some more!

They set up websites, and they talk! They hold more meetings . . . and talk! When someone mentions that they should, at some point, get around to actually *doing* something (p.s. mentioning = talking), they talk about drafting resolutions! And then they have more meetings and talk about what resolutions they should draft!

Sometimes they actually get as far as drafting a couple. But then some small group way at the end of the conference table starts talking about how this resolution or that one is worded inappropriately (drafting and wording = talking). Half the people in the room will immediately agree with this small, irked group, and the other half will be pissed that they even said anything in the first place (saying = talking).Then they'll all argue for another five hours, days, weeks . . . whatever it takes (arguing = talking)!

Eventually someone will stand up and sign, "Can we please stop *talking!*" And what that person means, of course, is that he or she wants to *do* something now. But everyone will immediately say, "See? That's internalized oppression, when you refer to our 'signing' as 'talking!' You're full of hearing values!"

So the offending person (the one full of hearing values) sits down, and everybody else goes right on talking. They slam their fists on tables (talking); they go "Eee-yah!" or "Hey!" while waving at somebody in order to try to get his attention ("Eee-yah," "Hey," and waving = talking) and then sign furiously at the speed of light (talking). They draft more resolutions (tal. . . . Oh wait, I covered this one already).

Finally they hammer something out that outlines (outlines = talking) what they "say" (cough) they're going to do. But nothing ever seems to get done. Which leads them to start talking about apathy in the Deaf community!

This is primarily why I hate oralism so much. Ever since it was introduced, you can't get the vast majority of Deaf people to *shut the hell up.*

He Wrote about Ring Bologna and Disappeared

My version of hell: I'm condemned to float around for eternity on a giant piece of ring bologna in a huge subterranean cavern that's half-filled with ring bologna juice. The steam rising from the bottomless depths sticks to my skin like a wet rubber hospital glove. I have nothing to eat except lukewarm ring bologna chunks, I have nothing to drink except lukewarm ring bologna juice, and there's just enough murky light to assure that I'll always be able to see my ring bologna raft bobbing up and down in the gentle lapping waves. . . .

I tell you this not only because I honestly believe that ring bologna numbers among the foodstuffs of Satan (which I do) but also to advance the theory that a Deaf writer can write about something other than deafness and not spontaneously self-combust. A lot of Deaf writers I know start out with the intention of helping to make deafness known to the outside world . . . which is a good and noble intention, to be sure. But we should (gasp!) also be writing about that outside world as if we (gasp!) already lived in it, because we (gasp!) already do!

Take ring bologna, for example. Does my opinion on this putrid, gut-wrenching substance somehow *not* count because I'm Deaf? Are there additional social or physical criteria I have to meet before I can write about ring bologna any old time I want to, just like a hearing writer can? And if I write down my opinion on this nauseating non-food, does doing so somehow make me *less* Deaf, since ring bologna has nothing to do with Deaf culture?

Or is it possible to remain Deaf and still write about ring bologna?

Hey, you never know. Ring bologna has lots of evil, hidden, dark powers that we don't fully understand. It could go either way.

Still, I think we should at least test it out: We could try being Deaf *and* write about things other than deafness once in a while. Just to see if lightning bolts don't come thundering down out of angry black skies, or if the pulsating (when we aren't looking) ring bologna in our refrigerators doesn't come creeping up on us in the middle of the night, entwine itself around our flailing limbs, and drag us shrieking off into the gloom.

So I've written about ring bologna, and now I'm going to bed. If I'm still around come morning, great. If not, remember me as brave and send generous monetary donations to my wife and cats.

Spleen Gone Blues

I met her in a bar
her drink was almost done.
Irony was hoping
that I would be the one.
So I slide up on the stool

and I say my pick-up line
I say "Baby how you doing?"
She says "Baby, you're fine."

Well wow, whoa
It was Halloween.
Who would've thought
she'd be taking out my spleen?
Invites me to her room
gives my knee a little rub. . . .
The next thing that I know
I'm on ice in her tub.

I woke up to a phone
set atop a little note.
It said "the market's good,"
and that was all she wrote.
So I dial 911
and I'm trying not to bleed.
I'm thinking economics:
"Supply and Need."

Well wow, whoa
her eyes were really green.
Who would've thought
she'd bring her own morphine?
She plays with her hair,

(Once again, I wrote about something that has nothing to do with deafness! How ya doing? Feeling faint?)

I'm checking out her rack . . .
next thing that I know,
I've got stitches in my back.

Now I walk through the park
and my eyes dart around.
Someone needs a transplant
and I'm the guy he found.
So he sent out an angel
with her hot, hot breath. . . .
But little did I know
she's the Angel of Death.

Well whoa, whoa, whoa,
she was firm and lean.
The sweat on my forehead
made a real fine sheen.
But through the operation,
when she took me apart,
she kind of left me thankful
that no one needs a heart.

Rubella Bulge

She said,
Because of the Rubella Bulge
there are more deaf people alive

in the United States today
than at any other time.

He winked and patted
his Rubella Bulge.

Footballs at $1,400 Each

Joe Boxer joined the Heuer Clan in the summer of 2002. It was a time of wonder, organized receipt files, and upright furniture. My wife transformed into Mommy right before my eyes, cradling him gently against her shoulder as she danced around the apartment to her Dixie Chicks CD. You would literally choke up; they looked so beautiful together. Mental pictures of him graduating from cat college and marrying a fine young feline flashed before my eyes.

Then of course Daddy went and screwed him up.

It started out with your run-of-the-mill father/son activities. I enrolled the boy in boxing lessons using this little Winnie the Pooh hand puppet I bought for him to practice on. At first, Winnie kicked butt; but within a year, Joe was three times bigger than Winnie would ever get, and carnage ensued. I was so *proud!* Amy would "Tsk, tsk" while the three of us played *WrestleMania* on the living room floor, saying that all of this play would go to Joe's head. But did I listen? No.

Where things really started going downhill, I think, was when I began training young Joe in the ways of football. This was around the time I got a new pair of hearing aids. Powerful things too—Widexes! Only $1,400 each!

Now, every aspiring football player needs a ball. So I would crumple up my wife's note reminding me to do the dishes (heh, heh), and that was our ball. Toss it and off he'd go—a natural receiver! When he started bringing it back and dropping it in my lap, Amy would say I was turning him into a dog. At which point Winnie and I would jump around whooping and chanting, "Dog! Dog! Dog!" Because Joe was a lean, mean, fighting football *dog*, baby! *Yeah!*

But now it's been another couple of months. Lately Joe has begun bringing his own footballs to practice. Two weeks ago, it was a credit card receipt (but at the interest rates these guys charge, do they *deserve* to get paid?). Last week, it was an old wadded up piece of Kleenex left over from my annual winter cold (but he used the tackling skills I taught him to tip over the garbage can. Don't you *have* to admire that?).

Yesterday it was one of my $1,400 Widexes.

Okay, okay. I admit . . . maybe this has gone too far. Kids need a father, not a coach. It's time for a bit of discipline in the Heuer Clan.

He needs that, you know? For hockey season.

You Don't Have 100 Percent
to Give

It's possible that my old football coach at the Wisconsin School for the Deaf (WSD) was not an angry man; but for a happy guy, he sure did yell a lot.

"I expect 100 percent out of you at all times!" he would simultaneously roar and sign at us. "If you can't give me 100 percent, then I want 110 percent!" Then he would drive his golf cart to the top of this humongous three-story hill that overlooked WSD's football field, get out, and glare down at us in the 100+ degree summer heat. Sometimes, for effect, he would add, ". . . *Goddamn it!*"

Now you might think that making us sprint up and down a three-story hill in full uniform was a directive meant to get us into top physical condition; but I never saw it that way. He was always telling us that football is a game of the Mind. When we got the ball, we weren't supposed to just lope around like orangutans. He expected us to actually use the brains encased (hopefully) within our helmets.

So as we lined up at the bottom of the hill to begin sprints, I did just what he said, and thought! Let's see: 110 percent effort at all times, multiplied by a steeply inclined slope such as this one, multiplied by the degree of heat, and factoring in energy reserves needed for pesky bodily functions (such as a beating heart), all came out to . . .

. . . death!

You see, you don't even have 100 percent to give, and certainly not 110 percent, and *certainly* not at all times. This is true both on and off the football field. These days, you need energy to even drive to work (ah, the sweet smell of rush hour in the morning!), let alone do your job! And let's not forget that running a healthy marriage requires yet more energy! And factor in kids? *Ha!*

Call me a wimp if you want, but I truly believe that my coach made us run that hill so he could separate the thinkers from the orangutans. I, at least, had enough energy left at the top to drag my ass over to the nearest water bottle. The guys who gave 110 percent all the way up the hill until they fell over dead . . . well . . .

. . . they didn't get to play football. And after we buried them where they fell, we finally figured out how that hill grew to be so big in the first place.

Those Who Play by the Rules. . .

Long ago, an invading colonial Army set forth into the dark, foreign depths of the wilderness to wipe out the remnants of a hostile native tribe. Every effort had already been made to civilize them, but resistance was ferocious. Captured tribal children refused to learn their conqueror's language in the special schools they were sent to. Captured tribal women could not be domesticated and taught useful skills such as cooking and cleaning. More often than not, they would set the cabins on fire or beat at the soldiers with the brooms they were handed.

The Captain of the colonial Army decided that enough was enough; something had to be done. It wasn't fair to the natives to allow the unrest to continue. Couldn't they see that they were destroying their children's futures? One way or another, more colonies would be built—many of them in these very forests the Army was now entering. It was the Army's job to protect the colonies. It was *his* job to protect the Army.

Years of warfare followed. The tribe suffered grievous losses. But they also fought smart. They learned to take out the officers. They learned to neutralize the advantage of cannon and rifles with close-quarters fighting. When the Army sent the natives bundles of smallpox-infested blankets during an especially brutal winter—as a gesture of goodwill—the natives retaliated by tossing their dead into the river that served as the Colony's water supply.

One day, the Captain, sick and weary from combat, called for a truce. He petitioned the native Elders, asking that both the colonists and the tribe meet—both sides unarmed—in a nearby clearing. Then the Captain's officers and the tribal Elders would sit down and talk . . . *really* talk. Winter was far from over, after all; and the food stores, both the Army's and the tribe's, were nearly depleted. Four-fifths of the women and children were dead. Half the horses were dead. Most of the cabins had been burned. And although the tribe could replenish its camp far more quickly than the colonials could repair their settlement, the Army hounded the tribe mercilessly, never allowing it to sleep in the same spot for more than two nights in a row. Everyone was exhausted. Surely there must be some alternative to the constant bloodshed?

The Elders agreed to this petition, recognizing its wisdom and truth. The warriors argued that it must be some sort of a trick, but the Elders disagreed. A man who could write words of such pain no longer had the stomach for war. It was agreed that the tribe would indeed present itself at the clearing—unarmed.

Thus it came to pass that they were set upon by the Army, which was hidden in the surrounding forests. The warriors were mowed down with machine guns. The tribe's women were raped repeatedly and marched off to the Colony's whorehouses. As for the children, their flesh was stripped from their bones to replenish the Army's food stores. The bones themselves were ground down into mush to feed the Colony's children.

What is the moral of this story? Each person will have his own interpretation—reflecting perhaps the horror of war or the bitter realities of survival in hostile lands.

But there was one Warrior who survived the massacre. Several days afterward, he crawled, frostbitten and starving, from the pile of his dead brothers that the Army had stacked up. I met him long ago in my travels. Over the warm glow of a fire and a good bottle of whiskey, he told me what I have just told you—no more. I don't know how he survived in the days afterward. I don't know where he found the strength within himself to overcome the loneliness and the horror—to walk such a long way, across so many years and such a great distance, and share that fire and bottle with me.

I do, however, suspect. I was overcome by his story, you see, and could think of nothing to say. So I asked him what message he thought I should take from his tale, what he most wanted me to understand.

He looked into the fire, and without hatred or bitterness, said, "If you're facing extinction, and you're still stupid enough to play by your enemy's rules, you *deserve* to be wiped out."

With that, he went to sleep.

Never Get Mad without Your Prescription

In 1845, Frederick Douglass wrote his *Narrative of the Life of an American Slave* and did his part to bring about the fall of slavery. Death threats would not deter the man, so great was his hatred for the injustices heaped upon his people.

If he had been alive today, he never would have accomplished what he did. His oppressors would have handled him with psychiatry. They would have labeled him Antisocial with Intermittent Explosive Tendencies. Where whippings failed, Paxil would have succeeded, especially when accompanied by forty milligrams of Ritalin so he could better concentrate on his cotton picking.

Now I admit that these theories are little more than educated guesses. And on top of that, they are based on observations of the wrong minority culture. I do not, after all, know for sure if a lot of Black people are given yearlong regimens of antidepressants because they happen to be angry about not being able to get a decent education or decent jobs.

I do know, however, that a great many Deaf people are given such regimens. Adjustment disorders and Prozac prescriptions are never more than a few steps away from their principal's or boss's office.

So let's be careful. We live in a world where it's easier to stick justifiably angry people on couches, dope them up with Zoloft, and encourage them to talk about their mothers.

Fiery as he was, good old Freddy might not have been ready for that.

Departure

What we'll do is depart
from the Daniel French school
of statue building.

Lean young Alice
right up over Tom's lap;
hair stuck

in his zipper, and weld
in flashing neon
cartoon balloons.

He'll say,
"Proudly Serving the Deaf!"
every time someone drives into

Gallaudet. She'll say,
"Yes! Yes Yes!"
A-shape suggestive.

Move On from Milan

The Milan conference is over, just like slavery is over. On the one hand, we've got twenty-first-century Black people combating modern-day problems. On the other, we've got twenty-first-century Black people demanding reparations for the enslavement of their ancestors.

Which group do you think is going to get somewhere faster?

Why Deaf People No Go Boom

I always get a good laugh out of it whenever I see how upset audists (along with the sniveling, collaborating deaf people whose minds they've succeeded in colonizing) become whenever independent, healthy, and free-thinking Deaf people protest something. No matter what the protestors do—write a letter, hold a rally, stage a walkout—every tactic is somehow always too immature, unprofessional, emotional. . . . The list goes on and on. Or else it's not the right time, or the right issue; the protestors aren't targeting the right people.

My favorite one is this: "I support the message they're trying to send, but their tactics are too *radical!*"

I don't know, man. . . . I don't think anyone has to worry about Deaf radicalism getting out of hand anytime soon. Call it an acknowledgment of bitter irony—but it's currently a running joke among a lot of Deaf people I know that if we ever tried to use *truly* radical forms of resistance (say, the explosive tactics used by Palestinian suicide bombers), we'd almost surely fail in our efforts. Why?

If a Deaf person drove an explosive-laden pickup truck through the front doors of a school that refused to convert from oralism to a bilingual-bicultural educational philosophy, one half of Hearing America, upon seeing the story on the news, would say, "See, I *told* you those deaf people shouldn't be driving!"

The other half would say, "Dude, I didn't even know they *could* drive!"

Making Deaf Awareness Day Effective

Why do we need a Deaf Awareness *Week?* Give me one day and your full cooperation. I'll show you more attitude adjustment in Hearing America than you've seen in years.

What we'll do first is buy a bunch of bicycle helmets. We'll put them on. Then all over the country walk into restaurants and slobber on people. We'll lift up our shirts and rub chocolate cake into our belly buttons. We'll grab ourselves (and them . . . and each other) inappropriately, shouting out with unbridled glee that today we colored a red butterfly and our teacher gave us a gold star! Happy Birthday!

Eventually someone will get pissed and tell us to knock it off. We'll stop our antics immediately and ask them, as visibly and publicly as possible, why they're so upset.

They'll say, "Because deaf people aren't mentally retarded!"

At which point we'll bow grandly and sign, "Exactly our point!"

Just Duck and They'll Shoot Each Other!

I've just spent half a book bashing stupid things Hearing America does with as much ferocity as I've spent bashing the Deaf culture for stupid things *it* does!

Yet I guarantee you, at the end of the day, Hearing Americans who didn't like what I had to say will dismiss me by labeling me a "Deaf militant." Meanwhile, Deaf readers who didn't like what I had to say will make that stupid HEARING sign in front of their foreheads (this translates approximately into "Hey, check out the deaf dude who thinks he's hearing!"—their version of "oreo") and point right at me.

Ha! What do you make of *that!*

Conflict

I have all sorts of friends who don't talk to me.

It's weird because these same friends "talk" to me all of the time, but only in the superficial language of "Hey Chris. How are you?" or "I'm fine. Have you seen *King Kong* yet?"

Then it gets back to me that so-and-so was mad at me three months ago, yet this is the first evidence I've ever heard or seen of it.

Fallout *is* a bitch, isn't it? You're left wondering—why do people, especially your friends, hold things back from you? Are you unapproachable? Or are they taking the easy way out by avoiding conflict? Plus now you've got the added complication of Friend #2 (who just told you that Friend #1 was mad at you). Do you act like you don't know? Or do you burn Friend #2's cover by approaching Friend #1 and making it known, subtly or not, that you now know?

What is it about conflict that makes us think we can avoid it? And what is it about the people we like, love, or at least care about that makes us think they're unapproachable? Why do we think we're not hurting ourselves when we've got something to say, but choose not to say it?

I can honestly tell you that most of the people I have known—past and present—have been annoyed with me on an almost continuous basis. I consider that an even trade-off, because they've probably also *liked* me on an almost continuous basis. I used to make the mistake of running around trying to make everyone happy. But I've learned that you can't. And you shouldn't. A person can't become a closer friend to you until he understands the depth of you: the complexities. The good and the bad. The only thing you really avoid when you try to avoid conflict is the opportunity to grow closer.

I wonder if maybe I can't ease things along by telling every new friend I make how a future confrontation with me would probably go:

Ideally my friend would come up and say, "Man, I love you, but sometimes I really don't like you very much."

I'd reply, "Dude, I feel exactly the same way."

Then we'd hug, or else we'd stay on our respective sides of the hypothetical rift for a while, slowly coming to the realization that we're having our biggest conflict of all over a point we agree wholeheartedly upon.

Nietzsche's Downside

What does not
make you stronger
will kill you.

Advice on Tennis and Pain

If you'd like to learn how to handle pain, go play tennis with your wife.

Get three games into the first set so the number of lobs wind down and the hard cross-court shots start coming. Get a return pattern going. Feel out weaknesses and strengths. Run like you're still 18 instead of 36. Or even be careful about it—it won't matter. Play enough, and you will get hurt.

Sometimes, you see, it makes no difference that you outweigh the other person by 100 pounds. It doesn't matter that you weren't directly hit by something. Not every ball is a missile. And not every volley is easy. Sometimes you're just out there moving around, setting yourself up for what you think is going to be a sure thing. Then you take a step at the wrong angle and *pop!* Out goes a knee.

Some pain doesn't hurt until hours afterward, or days, or years. It depends. What starts out as a throb at noon can feel like an unfinished amputation by midnight. Sometimes, what feels like fresh pain is really just old wounds getting raked again. Sometimes it doesn't have anything to do with the person on the other side of the court, with that particular shot, that particular racket, or that particular ball. Some pain is just saved up by God for certain random days. All the days we didn't feel pain were really blessings we didn't recognize, because for some stupid reason, we never consider ourselves lucky when we get a day where we don't feel it. Every now and then, a random Pain Day is necessary to remind us not to be so stupid.

To responsibly handle pain, stop playing immediately. Ignore your friends' shouts of, "Wimp! Walk it off!" I guarantee those types of friends won't be around when you're in a wheelchair. Go home and get some ice (ice is better than aspirin because what you put *on* your body is usually less of a long-term mistake than what you put *in* your body). Rest. Elevate. Check for swelling, not only in your limbs, but also in your head. Strangely enough, a swelled limb slows us down and keeps us away from danger—a swelled head speeds us up and makes us run smack into it.

And finally, get back out on the court as soon you reasonably can. Any day that isn't a hurricane is a great day for tennis. Too many of those days spent on the couch hugging your pillow will see you dead from a heart attack. Which obituary would you rather have—"Died watching a rerun of *ER*," or "Died diving for one more shot?"

I don't know about you. But for me?

Easy choice.

Missing the Bounce

Every now and then, a Deep Zen Moment will happen to me. I like to think of it as Life's little way kicking me back on track.

First some background: I recently decided to end an eight year friendship, and the decision wasn't easy on me. But what can you do? People change, even those you once called brothers. One day you wake up and realize that the people you loved eight years ago have become strangers somewhere along the road. They don't value you as they once did, and you can see it in their eyes . . . the fall from *that* to *this*. You wake up and realize—although there are some people you can let go of without a sense of injury or even deep loss, there are some people you just can't.

And it hurts. It shouldn't—you should be stronger. You should be more easygoing, more mature, more understanding. Live and let live, hold your silence, keep the peace. But it hurts. And because the only way to make it stop hurting is to end it . . .

. . . you end it.

When I'm upset, I take long walks. This is easier on my wife. I fall into terrible silences that move across the room like a black storm front. Amy will ask, "Hon, what's bothering you?" I never know what to tell her. Why do things end? Why do people go away? Why can't I just let things go? Life is full of loss. Why can't I get used to it?

There's a park that I walk to. . . . It's behind this old schoolhouse just outside of Old Town, Alexandria. I like to go and sit on the swing and sway back and forth. This keeps things Zen: back, forth. Stretch your legs, fold them back. More energy? Higher. Less energy? Lower. The changes in speed are up to you. When you stop is up to you. You get some control back over your crazy life when you swing.

On this particular walk, I found an old baseball half buried in the ground.

It was still in pretty good shape. Muddy and grassy-colored, yes; but it didn't have to pass any baseball polishing inspections within the next half hour. I tossed it up in the air and it went up fine. . . . I bounced it on the sidewalk and it bounced back just fine. That was good enough for me. It occurred to me that the ball might be some dog's ex-chew toy and covered with dried slobber, but that was fine too.

For nine blocks, this ball kept me company. Toss it and catch it, bounce it and catch it. It's like swinging back and forth. Deep Zen Moments are Life reduced to doing without thinking. When the alternative is thinking and thinking and obsessively *thinking*, you understand the attraction.

To illustrate: On the way home, my mind started wandering. I thought of taking the ball into the kitchen and washing it off with antibacterial soap. Give it a good scrubbing, make it *my* ball. I could carry it around with me at work—take a break between classes to play catch with a student somewhere or just toss it against a wall or something. It'd be cool. . . . People would see me playing with the ball and say, "Oh hey, look, it's that English teacher who. . ."

I was so absorbed in building a future relationship with this old ratty baseball that I wasn't ready when it came up from the next bounce at an odd angle. Nothing huge, not an arc I normally couldn't handle—it's just that at this particular time, my mind was a whole semester into the future. When I finally blinked back into the present, the ball was sailing past my fingertips. I missed it by an inch. It went by me and started heading back down toward the pavement for a second bounce. My eyes followed it, mentally computing its trajectory so I could go after it.

The thing is . . . it was heading right toward the only sewer opening on the block, one of those little rectangular holes built into the curb so the rainwater can drain away. Is it a coincidence that these things are just high enough to accommodate rolling baseballs? I think not. Somewhere out there is a sadistic rain drain gutter designer with a passionate hatred for children who play in the streets.

I was so shocked by this—I had missed the ball in the *one* place on the whole street where there was a sewer opening—that I didn't go after it until a split second too late. It bounced a third time and rolled right through: The perfect hockey goal, three-point basket, bowling strike, arrow in the bull's-eye, eye–hand coordination wonder. It could have been on one of those *Sports Illustrated* videos. You had to be there.

Boom, just like that. Gone.

My shock only lasted a moment. After a short pause and a grunt of disgust, I shrugged it off and kept walking toward home. But then the full impact of what had just happened hit me, and I burst out laughing. First rueful, then bitter, then sweet, appreciative, understanding laughter.

Why do things end? Here's the Deep Zen Moment answer to that question: Some things you get to enjoy for a lifetime, and some things you only get to enjoy for nine blocks. It's when your mind starts drifting to (and inevitably worrying about) the future that you invariably screw up the bounce.

And then everything rolls into the sewer.

Institutionalized Just Like You

People are always taken aback when I tell them that I was institutionalized. In their minds, *institution* equals *asylum*. Hence their discomfort. What *I* mean is that I was enrolled in the Wisconsin School for the Deaf (WSD) from 1984 to 1986.

"You mean you were *placed in a residential school*," they tell me, chuckling lightly.

"A residential school *is* an institution," I reply.

In fact, pretty much everything built by humankind is an institution. A church, for example, is an institution in both the physical and abstract sense (i.e., the Church). You don't technically even need an institution (a building) to put your institution (an organization) in, just to have an institution (an abstract concept).

You can place the abstract institution of Deaf education in any number of concrete school buildings, residential or mainstream. But is an unemployed graduate student writing a paper on literacy rates among deaf children any *less* a part of that institution simply because he's writing on a laptop in Starbucks? No. In what physical building would you place the institution of marriage? My wife and I got married seven years ago. Did I stop being married to her the second we left the actual, physical church we were married in? Of course not. And how would we even begin to discuss the abstract institution of marriage, the challenges of growing together over the course of time, raising kids, and saving for retirement, if we first had to gather all married people into the same building?

If there's anything at all odd about telling people I was institutionalized, it's in the fact that I confine my definition of the term to the two years I attended WSD. The truth is that I've been institutionalized my whole life, over and over, and so have you. Chances are you were born in a hospital, an institution. If you came to believe that a hospital was the place to go when you became sick, then you're a firm believer in the institution of medicine. You were (hopefully) born into a family, yet another institution. If you've ever voted: Congratulations! You're an integral part of the great, grand institution of democracy!

"Yes Chris," people say, "but it *still* sounds like you mean you were tossed in a nut house."

"Name one institution that, over time, *didn't* become a nut house?" I ask.

" . . . good point."

Dishes Done, Institution-Style!

My wife at times accuses me of not doing the dishes often enough. I defend myself by responding that any job worth doing deserves to be done carefully and properly. And if there's one thing I've learned over the years from working in various institutions for deaf people, it's this: Anything that you want done carefully and properly requires the learned deliberations of at least one committee, and quite possibly several.

I'll explain. Amy wants the dishes done. Check. Being an institutional man, my first move is to gather the remaining members of the Heuer Clan (in this case, our cats Joe and Raj) to form a Dishwashing Committee. From there, a Chair must be elected (such an action preserves within our internal daily endeavors the foundations of democracy upon which this noble country rests). Usually the elected Chair turns out to be the person who thought up the idea of forming the committee in the first place, unless the question of qualification arises. Such issues are then usually resolved by a motion calling for the submission (by all nominees) of a vita outlining one's qualifications for the position. At this point, a subcommittee must be formed to review the vitae submitted, and the subsequent analysis usually eats up about a week's worth of manpower hours.

Once a Chair is elected to run the Dishwashing Committee, it is standard practice to dissolve the Vitae Analysis Committee in order to free up those members for further duties. Thus having been elected Chair, I pull Raj and Joe out of the paperwork and assign them Vice Chairmanships on the Water and Soap Committees, respectively. The purpose of these subcommittees is to gather data on the feasibility of the project we propose to undertake (in layman's terms—if water, for example, is unavailable at the present time, or if it is available only from the bathroom tub, but not from the kitchen sink, that would put something of a downer on our plan to wash the dishes, dig?). Such studies can consume another week's worth of manpower hours, especially since data must be collected using a scientifically rigid and statistically valid apparatus. Time must also be allotted for the cats to present their findings in an open and transparent forum (which the Chair shall then review).

At times, communication between various subcommittees can collapse due to a lack of shared common dialogue amongst the fields of expertise represented. Raj, for example, with her chemistry/physics-oriented background, might pose a question regarding the molecular stability of the soap when exposed to hydrogen cascade effects. Joe, with his rough-n-tumble theater/drama background, might not immediately "get" that hydrogen cascade effects = running water. The resultant screwups in communication send both cats hissing and snarling back to their respective offices, where they avoid one another for the remainder of the semester.

The point I'm trying to make is that these breakdowns consume yet more time! As Chair of the Dishwashing Committee, I'm constantly running around putting out fires! And I just wish Amy would understand this! Especially since last night, she came home, found a pile of as-yet-undone dishes, and pointed out (somewhat unprofessionally I might add) that our kitchen was beginning to stink "like a dead polar bear."

What can I do? This morning, I assigned to Joe the extra duties of running the Stench Subcommittee, and already he's grumbling about it.

Research—The Best Way to Avoid Real Answers

I'm a dissertation away from a Ph.D. in adult literacy and educational counseling, so trust me when I tell you I no longer breathe oxygen—I breathe research statistics. I no longer eat food—I eat research papers (and drink the black typewriter ink they are printed in). When I sleep, I dream of setting alpha levels and checking for Type II errors.

Not that this is a good, or even normal, thing. But you make sacrifices when you go after advanced degrees: in time, energy, and sanity. You tell yourself that you're giving these things up to become a top expert in your field, to effect real changes within the System . . . that you can really help people if you could just learn a little bit more.

But the longer you work in the field, the sooner you come to the realization that the game is not being played in the way you were trained to expect it would be. Deaf education is not overflowing with administrators and teachers dying to implement the latest findings into their programs. Something else entirely is going on, and once you recognize *why*, you're forced to make an additional sacrifice: your belief that the whole point of research is to answer questions.

This is hard to do, because appearances are deceiving. Research articles *start out* listing questions they're supposedly going to answer. Prior research is reviewed, methods of data analysis are listed, the whole shebang. There will even be a clearly marked "Conclusions" section where the answers to the previously stated questions are supposed to turn up. But within this section, you'll find curious terms such as *a significant percentage*. Not *all* or *none* or *some* or *most*. No researcher worth his salt will allow himself to be cornered on this one.

Parent: I'm confused. Will this approach help my kid or not?

Researcher: The approach has been shown to help a significant percentage of students.

Parent: Well, is that good or bad? Will it help my child?

Researcher: I'd have to test him to see.

You'll also find a section entitled "Suggestions for Future Research." The purpose of this section is to provide a wordily camouflaged backdoor through which the researcher can duck if, when tested in the real world, any of his tentative conclusions fall flat on their faces. In this section, he will oh-so-delicately tell you that, while he rigorously and meticulously cataloged the discrepancies between the performances of Groups A and B, there is a dire need to rigorously catalog the data for Groups C and D as well. But he didn't do that, because that was beyond the scope of his study.

After a while, you understand that the primary purpose of research is to generate more research. It's meant to wave red flags and shout, "Look! We need to understand *this* better!" or "We need to study *this* further!" Research is meant to give professors something to argue about at seminars. If something goes wrong, it allows doctors, administrators, and teachers to sit down with parents and say, "Well, we based our decision on what we knew about best practices *at that time.*"

Translation: plausible deniability.

The Sign for Administrator

Pay attention, ASL students—here's how you do it: Make two finger pistols; first with your right hand; now with your left. Place them one inch from your temples. Wag your head between the barrels. All done!

No doubt I've just angered all administrators of integrity with the above idea. I'm sorry, but your anger is evidence that you probably aren't the kind of administrator Deaf education is looking for. Personally, I blame the job postings.

They should specify, right in the first sentence, that the opening is for a *colonial* administrator.

When Your Cat Is Passive-Aggressive

I am just so friggin' *glad* that people are not like cats! Take my cat Raj, for example. Passive-aggressive as the sky is blue. Currently she's mad at me because, if you can dig this, she has a urinary tract infection!

I know! The whole thing—impossible! But that's Raj for you. I mean, she's sick! Of *course* I gotta take her to the vet! And unfortunately this requires sticking her in the cat-carrying cage she hates so much and lugging her to a veterinary waiting room filled with sick dogs! Do I have a choice? *No!* And that's what I wish she would understand!

Because Raj does love me, you see. And she depends on me. In many ways, that's her biggest problem. When you depend on someone even a little bit, it can get kind of hard to express anger toward him. What if he gets mad at you in return and takes off? Or worse, what if he punishes you? Would *you* express anger toward someone who—the second you complain about a pesky little urinary tract infection—bam . . . shoves you in a cat cage and tosses you into a waiting room full of sick dogs?

I think not.

Thus, amongst cats, expressions of resentment and hostility are often disguised within expressions of love. Last night, for example, I was lying on the couch having a beer. Who else should jump up on my chest but the lovely young Rajah, who likes to curl up against my neck and purr against my throat? A pleasing sensation 99.9 percent of the time! Except last night was one of those .01 percent passive-aggressive times! Translation: When she jumped on my chest, she used her claws!

That's why I'm glad people aren't like that . . . backstabbing you with a smile, kicking your ass with an "I love you." With Raj, I can walk the fine line of never knowing if I'm going to get a purr against my neck or have my throat ripped out. But with *people?* I don't think I could handle that, man. If people were as passive-aggressive as Raj, they'd show up at committee meetings, shoot down every new idea, and then bitch about workplace apathy a week later. Or else they'd avoid learning sign language during the eighteen years I actually lived in the same house with them, and only then, *after* I moved out of the state, they'd finally take some classes. To show their *support.*

Tonight I notice Raj has clawed my new issue of *Maxim* to shreds. She's sitting in the midst of the pile of ripped paper with an expression that says, "How could you even *think* I'd deliberately rip up your favorite magazine? I would *never* do that to you! I *love* you! Why can't you *trust* me?"

I swear; the effect is hypnotic. I feel compelled to reach out, stroke her fur. Comfort her. Apologize for whatever it was that I did wrong. And she looks like she would welcome these actions! But then my hand just barely makes contact with her ear, and she "accidentally" bites my finger. She has a urinary tract infection, you see, and I should have known better than to disturb her rest.

Insensitive jerk that I am.

Invalidation

The Mind-Game Gift
That Keeps on Giving!

Hey boys and girls! Here's a nifty little trick that you can use in your next fight with your husband, girlfriend, beer buddy, or employee! It's called Invalidation! How does it work? Well, gather 'round and I'll show you!

Now watch closely—it's a formula! To strip people of their power, you must first:

1) acknowledge their argument (this proves you're a selfless and noble human being!)
2) say *but* (or some other negating/opposing equivalent word!)
3) reduce them somehow! And then . . .
4) . . . negate the reduction itself!

Sound complicated? It's not! Observe!

"Yeah, I think gay people should have the same rights as anyone. But marriage is about creating children too, and gay people can't naturally do that! Besides, all those protestors are from the San Francisco/Washington Bay area, and everybody *knows* how freaky they are! There are decent, quiet gay people from other places who have lived with their partners for years and are perfectly content to not be married!"

Yikes, hey? Here's another example. . . .

"Look, Deaf people may have a right to advocate for ASL in the schools, but all they do is complain! And this whole thing is just another example of how those wacko Deaf militants obsessively hang onto their own little worldview without ever thinking about the bigger picture! They're never going to be satisfied—they were all nuts to begin with!"

Neat, isn't it? In fact, you don't even have to settle for reducing people to small extremist groups! You can reduce them to just one person! To do so, for steps #3 and #4, simply say this instead:

". . . and besides, *you're* the only one who seems to have a problem with this! Maybe you should think about that a little bit!"

And if you really want to make the person you're arguing with doubt his sanity, after making the above argument, finish up by clasping your opponent's shoulder with deep concern! Look directly into his eyes and say, "But you *know* I'm your friend and I love you, man! I'm with you all the way!"

See? It's perfect! As far as Mind Games go, Invalidation cannot be beaten!

Institutions *for* the Deaf? Pfft

There's no such thing as an educational program *for* the deaf. From what I've seen, the primary purpose of these programs is to generate paychecks *for* their employees.

I've no doubt just angered all Deaf education employees of integrity. I'm sorry, but your anger is evidence that you probably aren't the kind of employees Deaf education is looking for. Personally, I blame the employee guidelines. They should make it clear, right in the first sentence, that you weren't hired to solve problems.

You were hired to perpetuate them.

Guys in Ties? One Tug Closer to Strangulation!

In a way, actually, it's fitting. Most men *already* walk around the workplace like they're dead. Why shouldn't they make a morning ritual out of sticking their necks in a noose?

Explain this to me: The first thing a guy takes off after he gets home from work is his tie. In fact, most men can't even wait that long to finally chuck the damned thing across the room. Want to know how to identify the car of a man? Look in the back seat. There'll be eight crumpled ties back there, scattered amongst the empty 7-11 Big Gulp cups.

Yet the guy who shows up for an interview without a tie is the same guy who will eventually go home without a job offer. And the guy who shows up for work one too many times without a tie is eventually going home without a job.

Why is that? We want to hire honest and trustworthy male employees, no? Yet in the workplace, we frown (and in many cases, stomp) on their not wearing the one thing 99 percent would say least defines them. Isn't a tie just a lie? If I don't wear one for two-thirds of the day, why should you suddenly trust me *more* if I alter my normal behavior for the remaining third (translation: the workday) and put one on?

Hell, the biggest advocates for ties aren't even *men!* I find it disturbing that the same women who have spent a century trying to wiggle out of corsets should find free-breathing males to be such a threat.

You know, I'm not asking for the world here. We *already* don't allow Black people to be black, gay people to be gay, or Deaf people to be Deaf. But I thought, shit, maybe we could just allow guys to take off their ties. The way I figure it, if the whole world doesn't fall apart after that, our newfound bravery might allow us to do away with nooses altogether!

And then we can all be exactly who we *are!*

White Dress Shirts— Making the World Safer for Workplace Projection!

Although I'm against neckties, I support white dress shirts. In any workplace environment, dysfunctional people will project their own unresolved emotional issues onto you daily. Therefore, from a job-security standpoint, you're far better off resembling a movie screen as much as possible.

Example: Last week, I wore my standard khaki shorts, leather sandals, and a short-sleeved cotton dress shirt to class. I did this because 1) it was hot out; 2) I dislike sweating, a condition usually expedited by draping oneself in layers upon layers of clothing; and 3) I don't feel any huge, pressing need to be dressed any different when I'm standing in the middle of a classroom than when I'm standing in the middle of my mushroom-laden lawn, garden spade in hand.

What happened? A colleague stopped me in the hallway and "praised" my outfit, rhetorically (translation: passive-aggressively!) inquiring whether or not faculty ought to be required to adhere to a dress code.

Now I will grant you that a teacher should at least *try* to look reasonably decent. In the spirit of cooperation, I have already compromised a bit on this point. If I actually *were* standing in the middle of my mushroom-laden lawn, garden spade in hand, it's a good bet that I'd probably also be wearing my favorite cutoff (at the shoulder, not the stomach—I'm not *that* sexy) Budweiser T-shirt. I have since learned, however, that cutoffs do little to protect my upper arms from sunburn, and I don't want premature wrinkling to mess up my tattoos. The artwork is very precise.

So . . . short-sleeved dress shirts it is.

That being said, however, let me also say this: I have been an English teacher for more than ten years now. And although I do not claim possession of anything beyond the most basic level of fashion sense, I do know that a noun remains a noun whether you're wearing a Green Bay Packers football jersey or a wrinkle-resistant tuxedo. A verb stays a verb whether you're wearing sandals, sneakers, or combat boots. You can wear an Italian pinkie ring or no—it's entirely up to you—but the adjective you're pointing at remains an adjective no matter how hypnotically the overhead lighting shimmers off your nail polish.

All logic aside, however (and in most workplace environments, that's exactly where logic goes), if you want to avoid the criticism of those who can't handle their *own* diminished-ego discomfort, don't mess up their movie (translation: projections) by wearing anything except white dress shirts.

This way, they won't become further enraged over the extra effort it takes to project onto something that isn't *already* a brainwashed blank slate.

The Tyranny of Polyester

Polyester offends me. That being said, let's examine the difference between my offense and everybody else's.

You can and you will get fired for having pierced lips. You can and you will get fired for having multicolored hair braids. You can and you will get fired for wearing shorts to the office instead of a suit on a ninety-degree summer day.

Come hell or high water, however, you will *never* get fired for wearing polyester.

I'll bet you a beer that I could show up at work tomorrow in a bright green polyester jumpsuit and not one person would utter a peep about it. Privately, they might question my sexual orientation; but they would never speak of this aloud. After all, it's (gasp!) *illegal* to fire someone for his sexual orientation. Just like it's illegal to fire someone because of his age or for being deaf.

Ah, but to be deaf *and* have pierced eyebrows. . . . That's a no-no all across the professional landscape of the United States. Deaf and *jeans?* Forget it, friend. You can have a Ph.D., ten years of experience, and a dozen publications under your belt, but if that belt is not holding up polyester pants, your next evaluation is going to be missing a few merit points.

I don't think that the world is divided into tiny little minorities called Deaf people, Black people, Women, Hispanics, and so forth, all of us fighting against the White guy. No, I think that there are just three classes of people: those who wear polyester, those who don't, and those who sometimes do. Nonetheless, *they* won't fire you, because they value you for the contributions you make, and not for your clothes.

If someone can be fired because her multicolored hair braids are offensive, then the overwhelming legions and hordes of aging, multicolored polyester-wearing professionals should be fired for the same reason.

But they won't be. And that should tell you something.

It's Vietnam All over Again!

Anybody remember Saddam Hussein telling us before the war that he was going to turn Iraq into another Vietnam? Bam—instant uproar on the Home Front. After that, nobody wanted to even *touch* Iraq. In fact, virtually every country we weren't getting along with at the time was suddenly being swept up into a Vietnam-comparison maelstrom. North

Korea? *A Vietnam waiting to happen!* Syria? *We should stay out of their affairs . . . like we should have done in Vietnam!* Afghanistan? *Not over yet. . . . It could still be Vietnam in disguise!*

Strange, how it sticks.

I don't mean to make light of the suffering and death that warfare brings, but exactly what is it that people expect? Is human nature suddenly supposed to change by tomorrow? Is there henceforth supposed to be eternal peace and goodwill? Are we never again going to bump into an ugly situation that unfortunately requires an ugly cleanup process? I'd like to think that as a country, as a planet, we're just a little bit more street-smart than that.

But no. Saddam knew exactly which button to push—exactly what to say in order to send nearly half of the United Nations into a "Hell No We Won't Go" frenzy. Even stranger is how the "lost one war, lost 'em all" attitude spills neatly over into a variety of non-warfare-related social issues. Clean up the environment? *Bureaucratic Vietnam nightmare!* Outlaw handguns? *Inner-city Vietnam!* Stem cells and cloning? *That's your medical industry ethical Vietnam, right there!*

Just last week, an acquaintance of mine had this to say about the No Child Left Behind Act:

". . . Jesus, now the government is pushing this, too? What they gonna do, send all the teachers off to jail if deaf kids are still reading at a fourth-grade level come graduation? They had a better chance of winning in Vietnam!"

I'm not sure, but do you think it's possible that over the years, all appearances to the contrary, Americans have secretly come to *love* Vietnam? It's our ready-made excuse to do nothing about anything, simply because we're afraid of becoming stuck in a nightmare of losing battles.

My Son, the Manchurian Candidate!

You can bet that, hearing or deaf, my kid is getting speech therapy when he's born. But the only word I'm going to teach him how to say is *Great!*

Reflect upon this simple truth for a moment: Most people do not want to listen to you anyway. They are merely waiting for their turn to speak. If forced to listen, they will usually (and probably overwhelmingly) prefer that whatever you're going to say be:

1) short
2) positive
3) cheerful, and
4) what they wanted to hear in the first place!

Therefore, it's hard to go wrong with *Great!* To further absorb the brilliance of my plan, picture the following scenario: My son becomes a spokesman for a major toxic chemical manufacturer. One day, his boss comes clomping up the hall.

Boss: "Heuer! How're those global warming stats coming?"
Heuer: "Great!"
Boss: "Good boy! You're presenting to the Board on Tuesday!"
Heuer: "Great!"
Boss: "And they're gonna like what they hear, right?"
Heuer: "Great!"

Twenty bucks says the Boss won't even realize that my son's answer to that last question makes no logical sense. The spirit of enthusiastic cooperation is so overwhelmingly *there*, why waste more time on him?

Plus I'm going to have a couple of backup systems installed in the lad. I got the idea from cochlear implants, believe it or not. What are these things, after all, besides surgically/technologically enforced conformity to the physical norms of the dominant social majority (translation: devices for turning deaf people into hearing people)? And since that lovely industry seems to be coming along so well, I thought I'd just expand on it!

Therefore, shortly after his birth, I'm going to have my son's facial muscles surgically altered to create a permanent smile. Then I'm going to have a microchip implanted in his shoulder. The chip will be designed to detect the approach of anyone who can advance his career and administer a mild electronic shock straight down to my boy's fingertips. The resultant spasm will cause his arm to spontaneously shoot out and shake hands with anyone he should ass-kiss! And all the while, he'll be smiling and shouting, "Great!"

Just imagine it! With all that going for him, how long do you think it'll be before I manage to get him elected President of the United States?

Engineering Efficient Institutions

Building still further on the concept of using cochlear implants to turn deaf people into hearing people, I've hit upon a great idea for improving our educational institutions!

What we'll do is genetically engineer all junior faculty for limited lung capacity. Since nobody listens to them anyway, and for their own job security, we'll only allow them to retain three seconds' worth of oxygen. In addition to this, mandatory speech training from birth onward will be provided, and it will teach them to say only one thing: "Excuse me. . . . I'm sorry, but. . . ."

Meanwhile, whatever lung capacity we take from the junior faculty, we'll add to the senior faculty! This, along with a microchip we'll install in the language processing center of their brains, will allow them to instantly identify the last name of any standing junior faculty member and bellow it out at 100+ decibels. Meanwhile, a second microchip (implanted in their palms) will administer electric shocks every time the 100+ decibel mark is reached, causing them to slap the nearest available surface. Backup system: Anything under 100 decibels will be covered in their own specially tailored speech training sessions. But the only other thing they'll learn to say is: "I propose that motion be tabled!"

Imagine how much smoother staff meetings would go!

Junior faculty member: (climbs shakily from seat)
Senior faculty member: "Heuer!" (slaps conference table)

Junior faculty member: (wheezing) "Excuse me. . . . I'm sorry, but. . . ."
Senior faculty member: "I propose that motion be tabled!"
Junior faculty member: (collapses back down)

Just think on it! No new ideas will be introduced, thus exposing the institution to only minimum levels of internal turmoil! Plus all senior faculty will know each junior faculty member by name, and parliamentary procedure will be observed at all times! The result? A crisply professional (yet refreshingly personal!), *stable* work environment!

It's such a good idea; I'm surprised that administrators everywhere haven't started covertly implementing some sort of program already!

The Lie of Dependency

In 1986, I was transferred from the Wisconsin School for the Deaf back to my old hearing high school. I was given an interpreter for only half of my classes. Yes, you read that correctly. We had two deaf students (including me), but one interpreter. The justification? Probably money—which is bad enough. What they actually told me (and the other student), however, was that we needed to be "weaned off of the interpreter."

Now this is funny. *Weaned off,* as if we were puppies, calves, or piglets. Weaned off, as if we were both suckling at our singular interpreter's breasts (one student per nipple).

Let me ask you something: Do you know the difference between dependency and interdependency? The first is a lie; the latter is beautiful.

What is a bird without wind? What's wind without a bird, or a tree to bend? The lie is the belief that things are separate from each other in the first place. They aren't. We cheapen everything with the term *dependency.* When we say that a bird is dependent upon the wind to fly, so what? The wind is dependent upon us feeling it against our faces—if we weren't there to feel it, it wouldn't be there either. It would go unwitnessed, the proverbial tree falling in the middle of the forest where nobody is around to hear it make a sound.

Interpreters for deaf people need deaf people in order to be interpreters. Deaf people need interpreters for whatever they need them for. The "dependency" on both sides is so far-reaching, so all-encompassing, why even call it dependency? Why make it into such a dirty thing?

Everything is interdependent upon everything—that's the truth. If you think I'm wrong, go live in a world where wind has no birds or trees with which to decorate itself. Go live in a world where birds don't fly and trees just stand still.

I don't know about you, but I don't want to live in that world.

And in a world where we incorporate the lie of "dependency" into whatever roles we assign to interpreters? Into whatever roles we assign to deaf people?

. . . I don't want to live in *that* world, either.

In the Depths of Space, No One Can Lipread Your Scream

Now you see NASA at least was smart enough to figure this out. They realized there's no air in space. They predicted that sound wasn't going to carry naturally through a vacuum, even if the astronauts flipped up their faceplates to cancel out any potential muffling effects.

That said, notice how *they* didn't strap their astronauts to a chair and force eighteen years of lipreading lessons on them. I doubt this was because they were afraid it would be too dark to see in space. Once you get up there, technically speaking, you're getting more solar exposure than anyone on Earth.

Can you imagine what would happen if astronauts tried to conduct a spacewalk using lipreading?

Space-Walking Astronaut: "Guys! Turn on my air!"
Astronaut Back on Shuttle: "What's wrong with your hair?"
Space-Walking Astronaut: (bangs helmet) "My air! Air!"
Astronaut Back on Shuttle: (to Captain) "He's bitching about his haircut."
Captain: "Tell him to quit screwing around and get the heater repaired before we all freeze to death!"

See? It wouldn't be pretty. A NASA dependent upon lipreading is a NASA full of frozen, asphyxiated astronauts slowly orbiting this fine blue marble of ours—a public relations nightmare, in other words. And in the midst of a media land-scape already punctured by bits of combusted space shuttles, the last thing you want is some orbiting astronaut's helmet (which he took off so his pals could see him better) dropping from the sky and possibly taking out a senior citizen.

So I figure Deaf education could possibly pick up a few point-ers here. It has been around a lot longer than NASA has, after all. . . . Yet so many of its employees still can't seem to com-prehend why lipreading might not be the best way to go.

You're Always Caught in Someone's Machine

In 2002, Halle Berry won an Oscar for her role in the film *Monster's Ball.* And hey, more power to her. She's a wonderful actress, and that was a really good movie.

The only problem is that 2002 was also the year Will Smith (*Ali*) and Denzel Washington (*Training Day*) were doing more than a little pre-ceremony grumbling about the fact that so few Black actors were winning Oscars. *People Magazine* picked up on the unrest. Even CNN did! The anger of Hollywood's entire Black community became hot news, and tensions heightened.

That year, a lot of Black actors won Oscars. Halle Berry got hers; Denzel got his. And I repeat: Wonderful! Good actress/ actor; good movies, both!

But did they *deserve* to win?

Somewhere along the way, you gotta have the guts to ask this kind of question. You can say, "Yes they did, but the White Machine would never have allowed it to happen." You can also say, "Yes they did, but it only happened because the Black Machine stepped in and threw some weight around." By *Machine*, of course, you mean the Hollywood producers and executives (with both conscious and unconscious racial prejudices) who have political (and public) pull.

What's weird is that both of those answers can be true at the same time. The White Machine can pressure for a *no*, and the Black Machine can simultaneously pressure for a *yes*. And vice versa. By the time any given Black actor actually receives his award, he has no way of knowing if he got it because the one Machine succeeded in handing it to him or if the other Machine merely failed to keep it from him. That politics might not be involved at all never really enters his mind. That he might be actually worthy of that award, all by himself, is a thought contaminated with doubt. In this world, in this day and age, he simply can't *know*.

Deaf people are in the exact same boat, not with Oscars but with jobs. Forty years ago, you couldn't get a job because of your deafness. These days, you might get a particular job, or you might not. Either way, it's *still* because of your deafness!

Place your hands on the interview table—you can almost feel cogs turning, turning, turning. . . .

Visible Scars

In my dream the old black woman
said, *"My, but ain't you an uppity nigger
for a white boy?"*
and threw a copy of the Americans
with Disabilities Act at my chest.

She said, *"What whip were you ever under?
What land did you ever lose?"*
Then she showed me her back, tugging down
the heavy sweater that protected
her oppression. Her scars were black

in the way skin visibly shudders
when ripped open, the way
melanin reasserts itself in fury.
I reached for my ears but could not pull them off.
I felt in my ears but nothing was there.

I wished for scars like hers;
to stand up and scream, "Look!
Look, look, look!"
I wanted proof to show her,
centuries of songs to the Lord,

a hearing overseer
with a whip. Rows of deaf men

in the cotton fields, singing in the sun.
Something you could see,
so I could point and shout,

"Look, look, look!"
She said, *"Don't bring your anger in here
to me, white boy,"* and pointed at the door.
I left the interview with a deaf man's guilt,
because I had no proof.

It Wasn't Self-Pity That Stopped Me from Becoming a Telemarketer

I often wonder where the line is between self-pity and acknowledging one's reality.

I come from what you would call a "working-class/poor" background. My father was a farmer until we lost our farm. After that, he was either a farmhand on somebody *else's* farm or a factory worker until the day he retired (when we didn't have any money, sometimes he was both simultaneously). My mother was a nurse's aide who often pulled overtime to help make ends meet.

That's hard work, all around. I don't say these things to brag. I say them to paint a picture of who my family is, and to honor them. We aren't lazy. We aren't too proud to shovel shit. We can take a beating if we have to, sleep for five hours, and still get up for work the next day.

But let me emphasize "if we have to." Unfortunately we *had* to—so what? If I could have made $8.50 an hour working as a telemarketer in college, don't think some sort of working-class pride would have compelled me to be a dishwasher at $4.50 an hour instead. I would have taken the job that paid the most money.

Unfortunately, the jobs that paid the most money involved talking on phones or talking with customers. Those were things Hearing America wasn't (and still largely isn't) built to allow me to do.

Now spare me, please, of your whole "Quit feeling sorry for yourself" thing, especially if it rests upon a foundation of "You can do anything you put your mind to." I *have* done everything I've ever put my mind to doing. Generally, anyway. I wanted to become an English professor, and I did. I wanted to be a writer, and I am one. It's just that I got where I am today by working on jobs that were a bit more strenuous than telemarketing.

Don't think I didn't resent that. Don't think I wasn't scared of running out of money. I was, all the time. I still am.

But is my resentment and fear *self-pity?* You might be tempted to say, "It is if you let it stop you."

Well, maybe.

But it certainly wasn't self-pity that stopped me from becoming a telemarketer.

If

What would the world be
if Rosa Parks
had instead gone to counseling
for anger management?

Grant Me the Wisdom

I have to tell you, I struggle with the Serenity Prayer quite a bit. Do you know it? I'll recite: "Grant me the serenity to accept the things I cannot change, the courage to change the things that I can, and the wisdom to know the difference."

I personally learned the prayer from Al-Anon when I was about fourteen. For those of you unfamiliar with Al-Anon, it's a support group for people sharing a part of their lives with an alcoholic. In my case, that was my Dad. In somebody else's case, it was a husband, a wife, a brother, a friend. The only thing we all seemed to have in common was this: The part of our lives that we *did* choose to share with the alcoholic pretty much resembled the aftermath of a tsunami. What wasn't dead already was instead buried, starving, and slowly dying of disease. And that disease was spreading.

I went to my first Al-Anon group meeting when I was four-teen. I'm thirty-six now, so that's twenty-plus years of holding hands with strangers and talking about our lives. In that time, I've seen a *lot* of parallels between the destruction wrought by alcoholism and the destruction wrought by other things. Audism being one of them. The general state of education for deaf children being another.

Judgmental of me? Sure. But that's how I've protected my-self over the decades. I evaluate things along a continuum of sickness and health. I evaluate *myself* along a continuum of sickness and health. I figure that as long as I can see the black, the white, the gray, and all the shadings in between, then I'm living in balance. It's a system that works for me.

But when I have conversations with people about deaf-this and deaf-that . . . pretty soon I might go: "This is hopelessly sick." Or I might be less negative and instead say, "Well this isn't fair; we should change this!" It really doesn't matter, if you want my personal opinion. People have the same reaction every time—they visibly shudder. Hell, they even attack! They say, "Hey, that's the way it is! You have to learn to accept it and not be so confrontational!"

Do I really have to, though? Accept it, and not confront it? Two hundred years ago, we had slaves, and now we have an-tidiscrimination laws. This was a huge social movement that succeeded in the face of overwhelming odds—it succeeded de-spite a *civil war!*

Would I be wiser to give up and accept things the way they are? Or am I wiser to keep on believing that things might yet be changed for the better? I don't know. Maybe the ultimate wisdom I'm going to get out of this is the understanding that nobody can decide that for me . . . except me.

The Starving African Children Ain't Got Nothin' on Us

You've seen it before.

You try talking to someone about a problem you're having. As soon as your emotions reach a level the other person can't tolerate, you get something like this:

"Quit bitching! Other people have it worse than you do, you know! Think of all the starving children in Africa!"

Now I, for one, have never understood the logic behind these kinds of statements. What, exactly, is the significance of starving African children when we're discussing, say, the crappy condition of Deaf education in the United States or the fact that a deaf person might have a harder time finding a job than a hearing person?

Don't get me wrong. My stomach churns right along with yours whenever I see those commercials of emaciated children hobbling along on withered legs no thicker around than small tree branches. It's horrible, yes. I give you that freely. I detest living in a world that allows such things to happen.

But you see I detest a lot more than just that. In fact, it's precisely *because* I detest certain things just as much that I won't be hoodwinked into believing that the one has anything at all to do with the other. I won't let myself lose focus or slip into apathy.

Take Deaf education, for example. For 200 years, it has been spitting out deaf kids with fourth-grade reading levels. You don't need a Ph.D. to recognize the truth of this. You certainly don't need *more* of the 50,000 statistical analyses that have already been done on everything related to the subject.

And here's another thing you don't need: 50 million starving African children.

If you think the woes of starving African children have anything at all to do with the woes of Deaf education, I will personally fly over there, herd a dozen or so into a cargo plane, run them through the lunch line at any state Deaf institution of your choosing, and fatten them right up. Then I will have met all your requirements: I will have stopped complaining and thought of somebody else in a position much worse than my (or in this case, my peoples') own.

Having met these requirements, you and I will then sit down and wait for whatever effects these actions (what *you* were talking about) are supposed to have on Deaf education (what *I* was talking about).

Bet you a beer we'll be sitting there for a long damned time.

Am I speaking too flippantly for your tastes? Then don't insult my intelligence. We are not meeting the needs of our own *deaf* children, and you're bitching about starving *African* children. Some of these kids are committing suicide over the stress of trying and failing to keep their sanity intact in our schools (and in their nonsigning families), and you're telling me other people have it worse? Is that what you plan to tell their parents? "Stop bitching?" If so, maybe the person who's speaking too flippantly is *you*, friend.

Then again, I could be wrong. Maybe the current state of Deaf education in our country does have something to do with starving African children. Maybe the plight of a deaf man unable to get a job in his own country is a less worthy subject for a graphic television commercial than is a Kenyan kid staggering around on wicker-stick legs. But hey, give it time. With no job, there's no money, and with no money, there's no food. Thus sooner or later, both American deaf children and African children ought to all start starving to death at the same rate! Maybe then both groups will get the same airtime!

If you want to solve problems, you have to learn to recognize "Quit bitching" for the social justice cop-out that it is. "Think of the starving African children" is a statement uttered by people who are inspired to order a large cheese pizza from Dominos whenever they see Peace Corps commercials on television. They say "Think about others who are worse off" so you'll go away and quit disturbing their Me-Time.

Therefore, you might want to stop going away. You might want to keep pushing the issue. Then you might actually get something done.

Life Is Fairer When You Get Mugged

To those of you who are so fond of telling deaf people to quit bitching about their problems because "nobody ever said life was going to be fair":

I hope you get mugged.

Have you ever *been* mugged? First of all, let me assure you that you're not going to fight back. When a person who is bigger than you (or not—a gun is a great equalizer) says he is going to shoot you in the head if you don't give him your money, your brain will seize upon exactly two thoughts. One is *Oh God, please, I don't want to die,* and the other is *What if he shoots me anyway?* That's actually good thinking on your part. In this day and age, you very well might get shot anyway.

Now, a quick question for you: Suppose you don't get shot and instead live through it. What's you're first action afterwards? Do you lock yourself into your car and call the cops?

Okay. . . . Why? I mean, nobody ever said life was fair, right? So what's up with all of your sniffling and blubbering? Big things prey on small things. It's the way of the Food Chain. So why should the cops have to come out and wipe *your* nose?

The bottom line is that you're crying and shaking with fear and impotent fury right now because you *do* think life is fair. It's just that you expect it to be fair to *you.* You expect the firemen to come to *your* burning house. You expect the mechanic not to overcharge *you.* You expect the doctor to find a donor for *your* failing heart.

And your money? That was *your* money! It's not fair that *he* took it! And your safety, to say nothing of your dignity . . . it's not fair that *he* violated these things! It's not even in question that you expect the cops to be there for *you*—they have to be! And chances are, if you're White, and if you were mugged in an affluent neighborhood, the cops are *already* there for you.

So why are you still crying?

You know, you're full of shit. If I try to tell you how, as a deaf man, my job is threatened daily by hearing people in half a dozen subtle ways, you shrug me off and say, "We've all got troubles." But if your tire blows out, you'll call Triple-A and get it fixed right there on the highway, thus saving you from the fun little jog that you would have otherwise had to take through an ugly neighborhood in the middle of the night. Life is so fair for *you*, you're never even allowed to get within a mile of anything that might shatter that illusion.

Thus I repeat: I hope you get mugged. Maybe if that illusion *is* shattered, you might develop some appreciation for what I'm trying to tell you.

A Message in a Bottle from the Governor of Reality (Hopefully You Can Grab This without Rocking the Boat)!

When I was younger, people told me to not rock the boat. So naturally, the first thing I checked was the distribution of weight around the ship. Something I noticed right off the bat: It had more than its fair share of heavy, useless crap lying around. I proposed that we toss some of this crap overboard. Then we might rise higher in the water, thus rendering the water-catching threat of "rocking" a bit less potent! But a crewmember informed me that the heavy, useless crap in question served to stabilize the craft. If we lightened up too much, we would pitch and toss and flail about in the first storm that happened upon us.

So the next thing I did, naturally, was watch the weather. An odd thing: On the days we did have storms, water would pool around all the heavy, useless crap, and we'd sink deeper and deeper! Because I wanted to stay alive, I grabbed a bucket and started bailing. But another crewmember caught my arm and told me that all of my rushing about was rocking the boat!

"But we'll all drown if we don't get this water out!" I screamed over the roar of the thunder.

"No worries!" the crewmember cried, pointing at the deck. I followed his finger and saw numerous holes in the planks. They were rotted around the edges from years of neglect and disrepair. "If the hold floods, the water will push up through the holes and drain back into the sea!"

Now, to me, this seemed to be a statement in blatant denial of the laws of physics (namely the ones written about buoyancy); but hey, I was rocking the boat. So at the time, I didn't say anything.

Another weird thing about the weather: On perfectly sunny days with a good strong wind, the crew never ran up the sails. One day, I asked the Captain about this.

"Oh no," he protested. "No sails on clear windy days, not us! We don't want to rock the boat!"

"But we're just sitting here!" I argued.

"Just wait 'till the wind dies down," he urged. "Then you'll see!"

So I waited. After a few days, the wind died down and the crew ran up the sails. The Captain turned the wheel as far to the right as it would go and lashed it in place. Then he called an assembly of all the crewmembers and asked them what direction they would like to head next. They got to talking, and I noticed that those who talked the loudest filled up the sails with gentle, manageable wind. In any case, we were doubly safe, because with the wheel lashed down like that, we just went in circles until the crew got tired of movement. Then the sails were lowered again, just in time for the next clear, windy day.

The last ship I served on was called *The Mecca*. It was supposed to take me far away to a Promised Land where I could live out my life in safety and peace. Instead it crashed upon an islet of rocks covered in seagull shit. After sitting there for a long time, cold and wet and with nothing to eat, I named the islet Reality and proclaimed myself Governor.

The moral of this story? I don't know, but I do have a question. If you're still out there on the ocean, serving on a boat nobody will let you rock even when doing so might save it . . . who's to say you're any better off than I am?

Man Up, Women!

I went to a diversity training workshop a couple months ago. I was one of two men (the other guy remained largely—and probably wisely—silent) in a roomful of about twenty women. The discussion ranged from White Privilege to Male Privilege. I learned, and agreed, that as a White man, I take advantage of these dual systems of privilege, even when I don't mean to, and even when I'm not aware that I'm doing so.

The conversation eventually rolled around to Deaf education. I opened my big mouth and said something like, "Yeah, but in good conscience, how can you criticize Male Privilege in the workforce when this specific field is dominated by women?"

Now *that* one drew more than a couple of looks from the crowd. "You don't know that," one woman said.

"Well, no," I conceded, "not for sure. But what's the female-to-male ratio in *this* institution? I'll bet you any money there are more women working here than men. In fact, in every Deaf education program I've ever worked in, most of the top administrators were women, and so were most of the teachers."

"But what does that have to do with Male Privilege?"

"*Nothing!* That's just my point!"

". . . I'm not following."

I sighed in frustration, trying to frame the argument. "What are the two most oppressive forces in Deaf education? Audism and paternalism. Any Deaf activist will tell you this." I paused then to let my next words sink in: "*Paternalism* meaning *male.*"

There was a long moment of silence while the room digested this further. Then the guest speaker (also a woman) spoke up. "So you're saying that since there are more female employees here than men, Deaf people should be linking oppression to *maternalism* instead?"

"Exactly."

"But Chris," she said, "who do you think women learned those oppressive behaviors *from?*"

I shut up. I figured she had a point there. Plus most of the women in the room were nodding deeply at the exchange, so I felt a bit intimidated. But I could tell that a few of them were as disturbed as I was.

After the workshop was over, the guest speaker asked me to hang around, and we got to talking.

"You don't buy it, do you?" she asked.

I shrugged noncommittally.

"Women sometimes internalize the negative behaviors around them," she said.

"That's true up to a point," I replied. "After that, it's an excuse. When are *you* responsible for what you do—bam—and nobody else? Including society?"

"It's not that simple."

"Bullshit it's not. It's that simple when you blame it on us!"

"On men?"

"Yes!"

"Nobody's blaming you!"

"Oh yes you are!" I countered. "Men started the whole ball rolling, remember? You just *internalized* it all. It's a joke—the fact that we oppressed you for as long as we did is probably the same reason you've never had to face the music for your *own* oppressive actions. But now you're in positions of authority, and surprise, it turns out you're just as bad! You just can't man up to it."

She folded her arms across her chest. "Man up?"

"*Own* up! It's what men say to other men when we're trying to teach them how to *become* men. Man up. Be accountable. Take some responsibility!"

Her lips tightened, and I knew I had gone too far. I had just met her a few hours ago, after all, and here I was blasting her with twelve years of frustration—twelve years of female colleagues treating me like a *man*, if you take my meaning. If you don't, repeat the word and add a hiss.

"I'm sorry," I said. "That's not . . . entirely fair."

She studied me for a moment and finally broke into a small smile. "I do have to tell you, Chris," she said, "I haven't met a whole lot of men who can *man up.*"

I smiled back. "There aren't that many, no."

Unfortunately, Now You Can't Get a Deaf President *Out* of Office

Let me start by saying that I do give you Deaf President Now protestors of yore at least a little bit of credit. You did, after all, not only demand that a deaf president be selected to run Gallaudet, you also had the foresight to demand that more than half of the university's Board of Trustees be deaf as well. By your thinking, that was a deciding vote—with a 51 percent deaf Board and a deaf president, surely the interests of Deaf people would now be truly represented.

But see, you screwed up.

Your basic argument was that deaf people can do anything except hear, yes? This is why they shouldn't be kept out of positions of authority. This is why they should not tolerate

---

Author's note: This particular piece was published on September 16th, 2005, in issue #113 of the *Tactile Mind Weekly,* well before Dr. Jane K. Fernandes was named the ninth president of Gallaudet University.

oppression in any form, neither through the ignorance nor the arrogance of others. This is why your president should be deaf himself, you argued, so that he could serve as a living symbol of this basic truth.

Unfortunately, you were right. I say "unfortunately" because I doubt you considered the downside. If deaf people are just like everyone else, then we're not only just like the best of our hearing counterparts; we can lie and cheat and steal right along with the worst of them, as well. Within us all, at all times, is the potential for corruption. Deafness is no defense against that. Why should it be?

Our U.S. government, with its system of checks and balances, evolved into exactly that form because our forefathers recognized that corruption is always a potential byproduct of unlimited power. To counteract this truth, they installed term limits in public offices. They gave other branches of government the means to override or reject presidential decisions.

Does anything similar exist at Gallaudet? Yes, if you're talking about the U.S. Congress or the American Association of University Professors or the MSA (Middle States Association). But I've served on Gallaudet's Faculty Senate. Let me assure you that my president (and once again, I am not talking about I. King Jordan, the individual, here. . . . I am talking about the Office of the President, which will be occupied by various individuals over time) does not have to listen to me. And neither does my Board of Trustees. I can suggest. I can propose. I can attempt to persuade. At the end of the day, however, there is only a Gallaudet president's deafness standing between him and whether or not he gives a good goddamn *what* I think.

That's all that stands between him and what *you* think too.

This is because during DPN, you decided that deafness was enough. So long as you had that, checks and balances, term limits, and popular elections didn't matter. So long as you had deafness, you could hand off a $500,000-dollar-a-year position (and instantaneous worldwide fame on top of it) and somehow still be forever protected from the realities of human nature.

Well, we're a young culture. And America learned.

Someday we might, too.

When Enough Do, Most Will

Human morality isn't difficult to figure out. When enough survivors of a plane crash in the Swiss Alps start eating the dead passengers in order to avoid starvation, *most* of the other survivors will join right in. When enough people start stoning a woman in the streets because she committed adultery, most will also start looking around for the nearest rock. Including other women.

Look at any newspaper if you doubt me. These things, and much worse, have happened. Atrocities are commonplace in our world. They cannot be denied. The primary defense of Nazi officers in response to overwhelming evidence that they tortured, executed, and starved Jewish prisoners? "I was only following orders."

Translation: "I jumped on the Jew-bashing bandwagon, buddy, just like everyone else."

Human morality is dependent upon an equation of critical mass. This is the real law that governs our behavior—not words written on constitutions, but the law of eyes and numbers. People watch others to see what they should do. They watch for the way the numbers align and follow the larger crowd. This is by far the safest behavior. Get yourself branded as a troublemaker or as a rebel, even once, and in quick and rapid succession (especially if you keep pushing it) you will lose your friends, your job, your home, your family, your freedom, your sanity, and your life. Where this process stops is largely a question of where/when it occurs and what is at stake.

Once a state of critical mass has been reached, once enough people in a given geographic location are doing the same given thing, that thing is usually labeled "right," and most people will do it. If there aren't enough people doing that thing, then it's usually labeled "wrong," and most people will not do it (or else do it in secret). If roughly equal numbers of people are openly doing things considered to be polar opposites, then "right" and "wrong" vanishes in a fog of confusion and debate.

The current state of Deaf education in America is an excellent example of each of the above three truths. This is also why the atrocities that it commits daily remain unacknowledged by the larger public.

". . .Anything Except Hear," Including Believe Inspirational Bullshit

I'm sick of the saying, "Deaf people can do anything except hear." How many deaf people can read this book? Give me an hour and I'll introduce you to ten who can't. I'm not saying this is their fault. I am saying, however, that this is true.

When it comes to literacy, there are two interpretations for the word *can*. In one interpretation, *can* is conditional. If you are exposed to an accessible language from birth onwards—and by that I mean *truly* accessible, something that you can absorb easily—chances are higher that you'll acquire the linguistic foundation you need to make sense out of the world (including all of the other languages in it). My ability to read and write in English is proof that, in my own case, this condition was met.

In the other interpretation, *can* is a lie. If you aren't exposed to an easily accessible language from birth onwards, then you won't acquire what you need to make sense out of the world, including the other languages in it. After a certain point, a million *cans* aren't going to cover up the fact that you *can't*. Anyone who tells you differently is lying.

Think I'm wrong? Fine, I will put money on it. But because it's my money, I get to be a bastard. I get to pick the institution.

I get to pick the students. To be fair about it, though, I will select only high school or college-age students.

I also get to pick the book, because mastering *See Spot Run* isn't good enough to get you a job. I choose *this* book. In terms of functional English literacy (something you should already possess if your parents and your teachers did their jobs), it's not overtly hard to read. It's even clever in one or two places. Plus it's mostly about deafness, and because the students I propose to pick will also be deaf, we should all have that "shared background/experience" thing going for us. So if all deaf people actually *can* do anything except hear, the odds are, at this point, actually stacked in their favor.

Nonetheless, I will win. I won't be happy about it, and I won't gloat over it. But if you still insist on telling them they can (even after I just got done showing you that so many can't), I hope God locks you in a classroom with them until you succeed in teaching them to do what you say they can. Every last one. Because the enormous group of functionally illiterate deaf people in this country is composed of those selfsame "ones."

Somehow I suspect that, if these students could no longer be shuffled out of your sight at the end of each semester, you might quit with the pretty political speeches and get down to the real work of actually solving problems.

Another Problem with "Deaf People Can. . . ."

Here's another thing I hate about the saying, "Deaf people can do anything except hear." What about all of the supposedly "deaf" people who *can* hear? I know quite a few who still have some remnant of that pesky sense left in their skulls. I see them on campus all the time, I-Pods jammed in their ears, practically slam dancing on the sidewalks.

This is a crime because. . . .? This excludes them from that hallowed group of "Deaf" people who "can" because. . . .?

Look, I really do dig the problem with the labels "hearing-impaired" and "hard of hearing." There *is* such a thing as being defined into inferiority (I never liked using either of these labels to define myself, even back when I still *could* hear something). Tell the average hearing person on the street that he's "Deaf-impaired," and he'll stare back at you blankly. To him, moving along the cultural continuum toward Deafness and away from hearing is movement toward something (even if only to gain a greater understanding of it) lesser than he currently is. And what's more, he cannot for the life of him understand why you wouldn't want to move away from deafness, toward him, by becoming something *better*—hearing.

So how do Deaf people choose to counter this linguistic subjugation? How do they reeducate the hearing world? Oh, I know! Subjugate hearing to Deafness! Hell, don't even acknowledge it! Hard of hearing? Hearing impaired? Bah! A person can have 90 percent of his hearing in both ears—nonetheless, if he chooses not to become Deaf (or even just "deaf"), he's shit on the bottom of your shoes.

It's got to be the greatest hypocrisy in the world that you've turned everything in your culture into Deaf, Deaf, Deaf, yet claim that it's all about resisting oppression. When hearing people oppress you, that's bad. When you oppress and ignore your own kind because they can hear too much—or even a little—somehow *that* doesn't count?

"Furthermore," you sign, "if those (makes sign for HEARING in front of forehead) people have a problem with it, the problem is in their own inability to understand and integrate themselves into Deaf culture!"

The problem can't possibly be yours, in other words, for doing to *them* the very thing hearing people do to *you*. Because, hey, you're Deaf, and "Deaf people can!"

Learn to Recognize a Smokescreen from a Smoke Job

First some background: When I was a kid, there was this Saturday afternoon television show called *Shock Theatre* that played sci-fi, horror, or kung fu "B" flicks. What made it so cool wasn't just the movies being played—it was this . . . guy.

He was the host (I never did catch his name). He'd come on right after the commercial breaks in this zombie/Phantom of the Opera getup, with pasty white makeup on his face and fake blood dribbling down his chin. His only job was to snarl and say, "Greetings, kiddies! You're watching *Shock Theatre!* Boowhahah!" My brothers and I *loved* that guy! Totally awesome swirling fog would circle around him in the background. He was just the *greatest* thing the 80s had going for it!

Ah, but one day, we wised up. The show went live during the segment where the Host was supposed to come on and go "Boowhahah!" In the background, we saw a crew guy running around waving a smoke-spraying machine—probably just a fire extinguisher.

Can you dig this? That totally awesome swirling evil fog the Host-dude was supposed to command? A freakin' lame-o fire extinguisher!

This is where the term *smoke job* comes from. The difference between a smokescreen and a smoke job is this: Normally honest people might unconsciously throw up a smokescreen when they feel defensive, such as your wife saying, "Well, you never do the dishes!" when you confront her over the seventeenth pair of shoes she just bought. One thing has nothing to do with the other, but with all the smoke swirling around . . . eh. Because the confusion wasn't deliberate, you kiss, make up, and life goes on.

But a smoke job . . . now, that's a different potato. That's where you've got yourself a lying-ass show that *knows* it's a lying-ass show. So it hires full-time guys whose only job is to run around waving a freakin' lame-o fire extinguisher just to dupe everyone else into believing the program *really* commands this totally awesome swirling evil fog.

Translation? Take the hearing parent who answers, "Well I gotta work!" when you ask him why he hasn't taken a single signing class in seventeen years—that's a smoke screen.

Now take the Deaf education (oral or manual!) teacher who—on the day the School Board Bigwig is visiting, grabs the only deaf kid in a class of fifteen who can read (the rest are still working diligently on *See Spot Run*), drags him to the front of the room by his collar, and makes him recite from impressive-sounding texts when Bigwig pokes his head in the door.

Then the teacher goes, "Yep we're all doing a good job here this year!"

That's a smoke job.

The Economics of Presence

Institutions for the deaf are dependent upon what I'll call the Economics of Presence. If I give you a quarter in exchange for a pack of gum, we're exchanging things of equivalent value. If the value isn't equivalent, this system won't work. A pack of gum isn't worth a penny, and it isn't worth twenty dollars.

It would seem that institutions offer the promise of education in exchange for the presence of warm student bodies (these bodies, in turn, are then used to justify and procure increased funding). The only problem with this theory is that institutions and programs for the deaf lack the ability to educate the bulk of their students (evidence: widespread fourth-grade reading levels), and they know it. For this reason, the "promise of education" is a poor medium of exchange for the acquisition of a commodity they desperately need: enrollment.

Thus, in the Economics of Presence, what's actually being exchanged is not the promise of education in return for students, but a carefully tailored public relations message. This message could be "socialization with other deaf children" or "an excellent sports program" or "a rich variety of extracurricular activities." It could even appear to be an education-based message such as "a challenging curriculum" or "a highly trained faculty." It doesn't matter—so long as the message itself can be tweaked to maintain the *illusion* of an equivalent exchange, enrollment can be purchased.

Therefore the most successful Deaf education programs are not necessarily the ones that focus upon the advancement of education. Rather, they are the ones most skilled at public relations.

Why the Deaf Education Teacher Went to Hell

Once there lived a hearing Deaf Education Teacher whose favorite expression was, "Your freedom ends where mine begins." She said this to her students often, and the older they became, the more they struggled to clarify their views and dreams, the more she said it.

If you had asked her why she said this so often, especially during those times when her students most needed to explore their independence, perhaps she would have told you that freedom of expression has to be tempered by respect and responsibility. And although this is a good answer, in answering she would have been just a bit too abrupt, a little too harsh. Perhaps this would have disturbed you, but probably not for too long. After all, there are worse things in the world to teach than respect and responsibility. Especially when one teaches deaf students.

One day after a long career, the Deaf Education Teacher died and went to Hell. But she didn't know it was Hell, not yet; thus she couldn't have told you why she was there.

For her, Hell was a beautiful thick forest with a narrow dirt road cutting through its center. Because she had nowhere else to go and nothing else to do, she decided to see where the road went.

As she walked along, she noticed that the trees and brush growing along the road began to thicken. After a while, she could not have left the road even if she wanted to. No other space afforded any freedom of movement. Thank goodness it was wide enough for two people!

After several hours of walking, she encountered a demon. But she didn't *know* it was a demon. Aside from an exceedingly large and muscular frame, he looked like any normal man.

The demon's bulk took up almost the full width of the road. She could only pass if he would turn slightly to the side, and so she asked him to.

"Excuse me," the Deaf Education Teacher said, "but I would like to pass by."

"Why of course!" the demon cried, bowing grandly. "You may pass by on my right any time you wish!"

And so the Deaf Education Teacher moved to pass him by on his right, but as soon as she got close enough, his welcoming arm suddenly shot out and slapped her upside her head. The impact was so great it knocked her to the ground and brought stinging tears to her eyes.

Sprawled in the dirt, the Deaf Education Teacher wiped her tears away and slowly stood up. "Excuse me," she repeated, confused and frightened. She could not believe the man had just deliberately hit her! There he stood, completely calm and unfazed, with absolutely no expression of malevolence upon his face whatsoever. Obviously she had tripped and struck her head. Yes, that was it!

"Excuse me," she said once more, "but I would like to pass by!"

"Well of course," the demon crooned and bowed again. "You may pass by on my left any time you wish!"

And so the Deaf Education Teacher nodded her appreciation and moved to pass by on the Demon's left. But as soon as she did, his welcoming hand shot out and slapped her upside her head, smashing her back to the earth.

Now the Deaf Education Teacher was scared. She looked behind her—the trees and shrubbery of the forest had mysteriously closed in over the road, blocking any retreat. She thought quickly. There was no way she could physically beat this hulking man blocking her path. She decided to try talking to him some more.

"Are you angry with me?" she asked, picking herself up off the ground.

"Why no!" the demon said.

"Why are you blocking my way then?"

The demon placed his hands on his hips, looking wounded. "I am blocking nothing," he insisted. "You are free to pass by on either my left or my right."

And so the Deaf Education Teacher tried again to pass by him. But this time, his fist shot out and punched her full in the face.

Lying upon the ground, bleeding and crying, the Deaf Education Teacher shouted, "Why are you doing this to me!"

The demon sniffed in denial, pushing his nose up into the air. "I am doing *nothing*. You are free to pass by on either my right or my left." But then he looked down at her, and with only the barest hint of mockery, said, "Just remember that your freedom ends where mine begins."

"We Can Save the Deaf!" (The Official Deaf Education Fight Song)

Their voices are a screech on a broken treble clef!
Assign some singing therapy to close up all the rifts!
Raising up my hand; piano to my left!

Tap my tongue, click my teeth,
and we can save the Deaf! (Clap!)

It's almost sexual, rub their little throats!
Add some clouds and shrubbery;
they'll bleat like mountain goats!
Touch their forming mandibles! Chins a tiny cleft!
Teach them signs for *ball* and *tree*,
and we can save the Deaf! (Clap!)

Put on plays! Work the script for days!
Let them run the printing press
and see how much it pays!
Brush their hair with hearing aids! We're daring
and we're deft!
Teach them to communicate
and we can save the Deaf! (Clap!)

Build them institutions! Sweeping dedications!
Teach them "yes" to nouns and verbs
and "no" to masturbation!
A tiny tummy tickle gives their lips a little lift!
Cochlear implant surgery—
and we can save the Deaf! (Clap!)

Their voices are a warble when they aren't at their
     best!
But strap them on a table, and we'll install the rest!
A few more statistics . . . studies with a twist!
The more we know, the more we go,
and we can save the Deaf! (Clap!)

On Being Brave

I'm tired of being surrounded by cowards. I hate them more and more every day. Always working behind the scenes; forever picking their battles. Always taking issue with how something is said, but somehow never around when it's time to speak up on the issue.

Oh, you have faith in them for awhile—but that's your own naïveté talking. Plus they're good at sounding brave. Their outrage seems genuine. But once you've been burned enough, your eyes open and you see. You realize that far from trying to resolve the issues that cause their outrage, they perpetuate those issues. They *crave* outrage. It's the drug that numbs them up—their perfect excuse for not doing anything or cooperating with anyone. It's their justification for looking out for Number One. They're too outraged, you see—they just can't trust anyone.

They can't trust *you.*

The harder you try to connect with them, the harder they will fight you. They will never challenge you to your face. That would be contradictory to the nature of a coward. Instead they'll sic upon you the Death of a Thousand Cuts. The problem that originally (and supposedly) caused their outrage is no longer the problem . . . *you are!* Now that you've acted, you'll never again be quite good enough, mature enough, right enough, patient enough, or controlled enough. With their criticisms, they will chop you into small, bloody pieces. Finally you throw up your hands and walk away in frustration—both from the problems and from them—and this is exactly what they want! They cheer! You can see it in their eyes, even if they hide it on their faces. Another good person giving up! Glory Hallelujah! Their outrage remains intact!

Friend, don't be like them. Don't. I know it sucks, and I know it's hard, and I know it's the loneliest thing in the world to be brave and giving in the midst of these frightened, small parasites.

Be brave anyway. Screw them. Do it for yourself. Know that there are people out there cheering you on; and I'm one of them. I wish I could give you more than that. I really do. I wish I could stand next to you and we'd face them down together; but you're there, and I'm here, and chances are we'll never meet.

Be brave anyway.

Do it because sometime long ago, you decided that you were sick of hard times and that you were going to help someone else out if you could. You were going to make the world *better.* Hold onto that belief. It's just and good. It's the first thing cowards and parasites will try to destroy in you when they meet you, because they hate you. You remind them of everything they gave up on within themselves so that they could play the game and feel a little safer.

Look at what their decision turned them into.

I Thought *You* Were KGB!

My grandfather's good friends, Karl and his wife Gretchen, were still living in East Berlin when the deconstruction of the Berlin Wall began in 1989. The citizens of Berlin (both halves) played no small part in its destruction, attacking it enthusiastically with sledgehammers for nearly a year until it was all gone. Rumor has it that this was the only way they could get David Hasselhoff to finally stop singing "Looking for Freedom," but that's a tale for another time.

As my grandfather told the story, near the end of November of that same year, Karl and Gretchen went to see one of the two new passages that were being opened to the north and south of the Brandenburg Gate. Thousands of East Berliners had already left the city, and quite a few already said that they wouldn't be coming back.

Lots of people were milling around that day, so Karl didn't immediately notice the man in the brown suit and sunglasses. At least not until Gretchen pointed him out.

"Karl, that man is watching us," she whispered.

From force of habit, Karl's stomach tightened, as if he could will both himself and his wife to become smaller, as if doing so could make them disappear altogether. The man's suit was just a bit too new, his gawking manner just a bit too obvious, for him to be either a native East Berliner or even an innocent tourist. That meant one thing: KGB. Hence the futility—one cannot hide from the KGB. They come at you from all directions, if you see them coming at all, and once their fingers close over your shoulder in that dreaded grip, you will disappear. Albeit not in the way you originally wanted to.

But that was *so ridiculous!* For one thing, Karl and his wife were hardly criminals or political undesirables. Nor were they doing anything to be frowned upon; hundreds of people had, at the government's invitation, come to see the new passageways. You could leave if you wanted to, and they weren't even trying to leave!

Still, in such situations, if you really *do* have nothing to hide, it's always best to *appear* as if you have nothing to hide. Thus Karl slowly began to approach the man in the brown suit, openly stretching his hands out in a "be calm" gesture. His approach startled the man badly, who began looking wildly around. *No doubt for your KGB comrades,* Karl thought.

But nobody came. No one closed in on either Karl or Gretchen to grab them and toss them into the back of a car or van.

"We're not crossing over," Karl said slowly, breaking the tense silence. "So we don't have our papers on us."

"Eh?" the man grunted in surprise. "Your papers?"

"Yes. We heard that anyone could just go if they wanted to; but we're staying, you see? We're just here. . . ."

"What are you talking about?" the man interrupted suddenly.

Now Karl was confused. "The . . . permits . . . to cross over . . ."

"I don't want to see your papers!"

Karl didn't want to ask the question directly, but he had little choice. "Are you . . . ahem."

"KGB? No!" The man suddenly began to laugh, relief evident in his expression and posture. It took him a moment to get a hold of himself. Then he said, "When I saw you both walking towards me, I thought *you* were KGB!"

My grandfather told me that story when I was still a sophomore in college. At the time, it didn't really have any application to my life. But after I graduated and spent a few years working in the field of education, I'd had a little taste of what an environment of constant oppression and paranoia can do to you.

That's why I laugh sadly when people flinch and cower away from the responsibility of standing up for themselves. "I can't possibly speak up," they say. "My boss would have my job if he found out!"

When this happens, I'll more often than not find myself remembering my grandfather's story. I want to shake these people by their shoulders and shout, "I thought *you* were KGB!" But if I did, they would just look at me with puzzlement. And I don't know how I would ever explain.

So many walls need to come down first, before they could even begin to understand.

Don't Stop with Dreams

Dr. Martin Luther King, Jr., had a dream. But I want reality.

I don't mean that I hold those who dream in contempt. I don't mean that I spit on others' plans to make the world better, or that the world as it is now is the only possible world.

But do you really think Dr. King would have been satisfied if his dream of racial equality could only become realized within the confines of his own mind? Of course not—otherwise what would have been the point of the Civil Rights Movement he helped set in motion?

If all you have is a dream, you don't really have anything. Dreams are formless until they are made reality. Argue all you want—I can't grasp your dreams in my hands, and neither can anyone else. If you don't tell me about them, or better yet, *build* them, then I can't see them. They can't inspire me. I can't learn from them. They are of no benefit to me or anyone else.

Now they may benefit *you*, and if that's what you intend, fine. But if what you want is to help people out, then you've got to wake up and get out of bed. Don't fall into the trap of believing that all you have to do is dream and then you're done. You're not. For every dream you fail to realize, for every reality you fail to create, those who could benefit from your ideas at best gain nothing.

At worst, they suffer.

I have a dream that deaf children in this country will one day be properly educated. I have a dream that the Signing community will rise up and shake America's Deaf educational system to its foundations, that they will shake it free of its current state of apathy and inertia.

This is my dream. I'm telling you about it so it won't stay a dream. I'm telling you because I don't want dreams. I want *reality*.

Strip Club Literacy

Every night, millions of international businessmen end up in strip clubs near American airports. It matters very little whether or not they can speak or read even a single word of English. From Japan to Hawaii (in either direction), everyone knows that Paradise Oasis isn't a fruit-drink store. The blinking neon Exotic Dancers sign isn't advertising night class opportunities for Apache Rain Dance students.

So how do we account for the advertising success of strip clubs? I personally think they do well because their owners don't have the same literacy hang-ups as do quite a few teachers in the American Deaf education system.

A lot of these teachers believe that if something wasn't spat out of a typewriter, it's not English. This may be why the last public school I taught in was still using dusty sentence-pattern textbooks from the 1970s with nary a picture to be found in any of them.

This may also be why ASL has had as many classroom-survival problems as it has over the years. That particular language isn't about actual paper and pens and print—we kept saying all along that our "paragraphs" were being "written" in the air, all to no avail. In the end, people couldn't make the leap. The problem wasn't just that they couldn't change the way they thought about deafness (medical malady → cultural identity).

They also couldn't change the way they thought about *text.*

I wonder if that still has to be the case. Today, a child can call up a paragraph about World War II on his computer, click on the word *Nazis,* and get thirty seconds of film showing Hitler at a military parade. That child probably learned as much from the footage as he did from the actual English paragraph. In fact, he may have understood certain words only *because* he could connect them to specific pictures.

Strip club owners understand this—thus the redundancy of the flashing neon boob-girl next to the Paradise Oasis sign. Hiss at the inappropriateness of the image if you must. But you can bet on this: Those are the two English words an international businessman will surely remember when he sees them again.

I say we go with what works.

(P.S. Did the arrow above do as good of a job as the English preposition *to?* I think it did.)

ASL Is a Visual Language . . . Just Like Printed English!

Why do Deaf people keep making such a big thing about how ASL is a visual language? I mean, it is, sure, but they empha-size this as if ASL is the *only* visual language in God's Known Universe. As if that's what makes it unique and special.

Now I bet you're going to leap ahead and say something like, "Yeah, I see what you're getting at, and you're right. British Sign

Language is visual too. So is every country's native sign language. It's a bit arrogant of us to keep emphasizing American, American, *American* all the time."

Well . . . true; but that's not what I was getting at. I specifically mean that Deaf people emphasize that American *Sign* Language is a visual language—as if printed languages, solely by virtue of the fact that they are printed, are not visual.

Okay, let's run an experiment. Read the sentence below:

Kiss my bald, pimpled ass.

That's printed English, an example of a printed language. Can you actually *see* the print? Yes? Okay, so that's score one for printed English as a visual language!

But wait, there's more! Using raw imagination, can you visualize my ass? Seriously, try! Let me use more printed English to describe it. . . .

Oh, you don't need me to do that? Okay, so that's score *two* for printed English as a visual language!

I'm not trying to detract from the beauty of ASL, nor the pride that many people (myself included) place in it. But if people are going to use the adjective *visual* for bragging rights, shouldn't they at least make sure that isn't something ASL has in common with every other friggin' language on the planet?

Let's Bring Back "Deaf and Dumb"

Why do you want to get rid of the label "Deaf and Dumb?" We're surrounded by all kinds of stupid Deaf people—it's the *perfect* label for them!

Case in point: Just last week, I was arguing with this Deaf guy. In ASL, he signed, "Hate English, me! Why? Stupid hearing language! Oppress Deaf, hearing! If English learn, me, encourage hearing oppress! Refuse!"

English translation (roughly, anyway): "I hate English because it's the stupid language of hearing people! Hearing people oppress Deaf people! Therefore if I learn English, I am encouraging the oppression of my own people! I refuse to do that!"

See what I mean? Dumb as a friggin' brick.

Let me specify something. In my experience, you can divide Deaf people who refuse to learn English into two general groups. One group is comprised of people who were never exposed to a primary language of any kind before the age of two—either English or ASL—thus it's not even a question of "refuse to." They *can't* learn English because they lack the linguistic foundation to do so. And what's more, they know this. So they cover it up with false pride.

The other group *was* exposed to ASL early on and thus *does* have the linguistic foundation to master a second language: English. Nonetheless they *won't* learn English because they actually believe the horseshit argument given above. That's the group I'm talking about here.

Tell you what: Let's reconstruct that argument using substitute premises. Instead of "hearing people," we'll use the label "White people." Instead of "Deaf people," we'll use "Native American Indians." Instead of "language," we'll use "weapons." And instead of "English," we'll use "rifles."

Now the argument becomes: "I hate rifles because these are the stupid weapons of White people! White people oppress Native American Indians! Therefore if I use rifles, I am encouraging the oppression of my own people! I refuse to do that!"

Hmm. Not bad, so far as the logic is concerned. Some of the points are even true! But think for a second. . . . If Native American Indians had started out possessing just as many rifles as the White settlers, would White people currently rule America? And if the Native American braves of yesteryear had actually made it a practice to ignore the fallen rifles of dead White settlers (rather than picking those rifles up and using them), would our current population of Native American Indians be as big as it is?

I'm not arguing that English is superior to ASL in the way that rifles are superior to bows and arrows (quickly, if you had to pick, which one would you rather be shot with?). But if I were in for the fight of my life—and make no mistake about it, Deaf people living in the twenty-first century most definitely *are* in for the fight of their lives—I would use anything I could to win. I would study the ways of my enemy inside out and use them against him, even if he didn't want to be my enemy. Anything that made me that much tougher to beat, I would take advantage of . . . no question about it, and no shame in it. What, do you think the CIA isn't currently recruiting every American-born Arabic- or Korean-literate college student it can get its hands on?

The bitter irony of this whole thing is that the above question is actually moot. The very people that it was meant for chose not to learn enough English to answer it.

Sometimes Things Break Off

I had a good job at the time. I had a lot of friends to hang out with. I had a girlfriend and a car that ran. It was a full life. I want you to understand this.

I also had a relatively decent roommate. He was late paying the phone bill once in a while, sure; but he was a ferocious birdie-racket wielder—a good guy to have around when someone is trying to break into your apartment.

It was 1998. Milwaukee was having one of its meaner winters. I was sitting in the living room of our basement apartment playing *Metal Gear* on the PlayStation.

All of a sudden Greg came running up. "What was *that?*" he hissed, clearly alarmed. His expression, along with the birdie-racket he was gripping in his right fist, helped me figure this out.

I paused the game, thinking I had accidentally left the volume on. But it wasn't the game. Greg was gesturing frantically toward the unlocked door to the entryway—a small hallway that led from our living room to our front door.

"Someone kicked the window in," he signed, making little kicking motions with his foot. "I heard the glass break!" His face was white with terror. . . . Believe me; I am not exaggerating.

There was no other weapon available except Greg's birdie-racket (unfortunately he hadn't bought a matching set). I yelled out to the intruder that we were going to pummel unconscious anyone we found behind the door, so now was the time to take off! We then made sure to give the intruder enough time to actually leave (birdie racket vs. gun = not a good idea). When it became apparent that sufficient time had been allotted, I slowly pushed open the entryway door and we peeked in.

A 250-pound chunk of ice had broken off the roof of the neighboring apartment building and crashed into the alley, blowing out our window. The floor was covered in glass shards and wood splinters.

Moral of the story: Sometimes you can have a good job, a lot of friends to hang out with, a girlfriend, a car that runs, and a relatively decent roommate. But then one night, out of the cold dark winter blue, without there being any predestined reason for it, a 250-pound ice chunk *still* comes crashing through the entryway window of your basement apartment.

It's the nature of giant ice chunks, and it's the nature of misfortune.

Parenthood in the Blizzard

When they were born deaf
it was the D.C. blizzard of '03.
Every means of getting anywhere
buried under five feet of frozen slush;
little American flags sticking up
off the roofs of cars so the plows
wouldn't hit them.

I saw more people on that day
than I had seen all year—
many offering sympathetic smiles
or shovels.
Route 1 is clear, they told me,
but the walks are a bitch.
Hopeless, because

if you want real help,
you need both the roads and the walks
to actually get in and out
of the houses. So the plows cleared
immediate problems—
you could barely find where you parked!
No American flag

is going to do the digging out for you.
No authorities are handling emergencies
on the small-scale. You can't stand in line
for an hour at the supermarket
and buy a pizza, all the while pretending
you're able to make do,
that if you had a cabin somewhere

you'd be a modern-day Grizzly Adams.
Could you really cope?
When my children were born deaf I saw
all the people in the streets
with dinky little plastic urban shovels,
completely inadequate.
Everything snapping in half.

Denial Rules Everything

I wouldn't necessarily say that I'm fat. I am, however, bulky in a semi-threatening sort of way. I will never play football for the Green Bay Packers, but I would make an excellent tackling dummy.

I approach the dynamics of successful weight loss from what you might call the loser's point of view. My idea of exercise is climbing out of my lounge chair to get a popsicle. And believe me, when I can afford one of those new chairs with freezer units built into the armrests, I'm buying one.

I'm quite fatalistic about the power of denial, you see. It rules everything anyway; you might as well surrender.

Can you imagine the expression on my face when I show up at the YMCA to do my first set of twenty consecutive jumping jacks in three months? You can tell I'm going to go home and weigh in afterwards. If I haven't lost at least ten pounds by then, I'm not coming back tomorrow.

A lot of nonsigning parents I meet have that exact same attitude. Their deaf child just turned twelve, and these parents are only *now* taking their first signing class? And what's more, you can tell they won't be coming back to class next week if they aren't signing fluent ASL by the end of the day.

I don't want to hear that losing weight and keeping it off doesn't come from doing twenty jumping jacks every three months. . . . It comes from permanently altering lifetime eating and exercise habits. Similarly, *they* don't want to hear that communicating effectively with their child requires more than one sign language class—it may require *years* of classes. But true to our upbringing in the American culture of instant gratification, I want twenty pounds gone *now,* and they want their deaf child understanding them *yesterday!* Otherwise who has the time?

But good luck explaining to them that it doesn't work that way. And good luck telling me that if I don't start exercising soon, my heart will someday explode in my chest.

Denial rules everything, you see; and I'll give you the same response that those parents will give you:

"Yeah, yeah. I'll get to it when I get to it."

Coping

I used to work with this kid, Junior. He was a pain in the ass from day one. He had no language ability whatsoever, meaning he could barely spell his own name. He was immature as hell, too . . . around anyone he happened to be with. Teachers, other deaf students, hearing students, you name it.

He also had absolutely no ability to tolerate frustration. The mechanism for doing so didn't seem to exist in his brain. With him, there was no gradual release of tension, no moving through various levels or gradations of anger. Piss him off and—*boom!*—up like a rocket he'd go! Tell him he'd have to do his math homework over, and he'd beat his forehead against the wall until it bled, especially if you didn't get there in time to stop him.

Believe me, that's no exaggeration.

* *

Anyway, Parent's Night rolls around. Remember, at this stage in my career, I was still a lowly teaching assistant. Meaning my job that night was to basically just rotate around through the various classrooms and chat with the parents while the lead teachers did the real consulting. This one teacher, Mrs. B, wanted me in her room at 7 p.m. sharp, because Junior's father—Dad—was dropping by to visit! I worked closely with Junior (translation: If I got to him in time, I pulled him away from the wall and wiped off the blood splotches), so I should be there in case Dad had any questions.

At 7 p.m., in he came.

"Thank you for coming!" Mrs. B said/signed. "Junior is doing very *well* and. . . .!" They were tight within fifteen seconds flat—a true masterpiece of salesmanship. If Deaf education ever crashes nationwide, more than a few of its teachers would do well as used car salesmen. They were born for the job, and it'd be a shame to waste the talent.

About ten minutes into Mrs. B's pitch, I figured I should interject a little something. Seeing how *closely* I worked with Junior and all.

"Hey Dad," I said, "are you aware your kid blows up whenever I tell him he did his homework wrong? He beats his forehead against the wall until it bleeds. He seems kind of frustrated to me."

Dead silence.

I continued: "Maybe if you'd sign with him a bit, he could communicate with you. And then he wouldn't be so frustrated."

Dead silence.

"You *can* sign, right?" I asked.

Mrs. B rubbed her eyes.

"Junior understands me," Dad insisted suddenly (and more than just a little defensively). And no, he *couldn't* sign. Mrs. B had to interpret for him while I glared at her.

"I'm sorry, but somehow I doubt that."

Dad smacked his palm on the table. "He does too!" he snapped. "He reads my lips just fine!"

* *

Maybe I should have let it go at that point. But for some reason, I couldn't. How many times had I walked Junior down the hallway to the school nurse's office so she could bandage his forehead? Ten times? Fifteen that semester alone?

On my very first day at that school, I walked into Mrs. B's room and saw this weird-looking phone booth in there. Only it held no phone, and it was made out of tough brown plastic instead of steel and glass. It also had a door that sealed magnetically and was very tough to pry open. Even for me.

"What is that thing?" I asked her.

"Oh, we use that for the unruly ones," she signed, laughing lightly as she fingerspelled UNRULY. "Security puts them in there until they calm down."

"You're kidding me." I was certain I had misunderstood her.

She stared back, not comprehending.

* *

"Hey," I said, "do you know that *Farside* cartoon? The one about Fifi?"

Dad shook his head.

"It's got two frames. One is entitled 'What Bob Says.' Bob's in there talking to his dog, Fifi. He's going, 'Now Fifi, I want you to stay right here while I go get your food! That's a good dog, Fifi. . . .'"

Mrs. B looked like she wanted to die.

"The second frame is entitled 'What Fifi Understands.' Only in that one, Bob is going 'Blah blah, Fifi, blah blah blah, Fifi, blah blah blah, Fifi. . . .'"

Dad stood up quietly to leave.

"*That's* how well Junior understands you!" I yelled after him.

After Dad left (translation: He slammed the door so hard, two lockers across the hallway swung open from the force of the shockwave), Mrs. B cornered me. "Chris," she signed, "what the hell possessed you to talk to him that way!"

I had never seen her so furious. Then again I had never felt so tired. "He's screwing up his kid," I answered.

"It took me over six months to get him to agree to come to a parent-teacher conference! Before tonight, he hasn't set a foot in this school for three years!"

I pushed her hand out of my face. "So what?"

"It's always Junior's mother who comes instead!"

* *

That whole incident put a bad taste in my mouth for the next ten years of my career. What, Dad's a great parent now, because he finally came to a parent-teacher conference? And getting him there . . . *that's* a big accomplishment? Somehow that justifies everything? Junior might have grown up well-adjusted. Instead he was driven out of his mind because his parents were psychologically starving him—daily—for communication. But that didn't matter, you see, because his parents were *coping.* And Mrs. B was *making progress* with them.

How do you maintain your faith in people when you're surrounded by this? I try; but it's hard.

It's really hard.

The Economy of Love and Paying Attention

It's a curious expression, isn't it? "Pay attention."

I *love* it! Everything costs something, after all. You pay for your pizza; you pay for your beer. Hockey tickets are still forty dollars for nosebleed seats, and the bikini girls of *Stuff* are yours only *after* you pay five bucks for the magazine.

But hey, that's okay. You understand. You were trained to think in Manpower Hours. This equals that—it was the whole point of elementary school math:

Teacher: "Tommy works for Uncle Sam for forty years, paying taxes all the way. At retirement, children, what does Tommy have left?"

Children: "Nothing!"

Ah, but then some idiot screwed everything up with Love. Love is free, you see! Love is patient; love is kind! There's no scoreboard; friends don't keep track! It isn't a competition and it isn't a war, except maybe for male actors in chick flicks playing cynical Wall Street yuppie businessmen who nonetheless melt and fall in love with the girl by the end of the show (the movie tickets themselves cost nine bucks a pop).

So I say *thank God* for "Pay attention."

This curious little expression brings us back to the nuts and bolts of the economic universe in which there is definitely *no* such thing as a free lunch. It's *not* true that "Love doesn't cost a thing!" It's just that instead of paying for it in cash (no hooker/gold digger jokes, please), you pay for it with attention.

Get it? What you don't pay for with attention, you pay for with . . . divorce! What you don't pay for with attention, you pay for with a screwed-up kid, you pay for in shattered friendships, you pay for in estranged parents, and you pay for in ultimately dying alone with nobody at your bedside to play checkers with.

This is why I have little sympathy for nonsigning parents of deaf children who explain away their child's behavioral outbursts with, "Oh he's just trying to get attention."

Well, *duh!*

In other words, he's trying to collect what they've probably owed him for years.

The Best Defense Is a Good Disqualification

I hate it when parents counter every argument made against the overall shoddy performance of Deaf education (especially the particular programs their children attend) with this: "Excuse me, but do *you* have a child in this school? Do you work here? Well then who are you to judge?"

Indeed. That's like saying I'm not qualified to criticize the quality of the air over Los Angeles because I happen to live in Washington, D.C., or that I can't worry about China's contribution to global warming because I live in America. Nor can I call Microsoft when my computer breaks down, because I don't work for them. It's ridiculous. Using that logic, it's absurd to blame even a single cancer-related death on second-hand smoke. Unless the victim sucked down three packs a day of his *own*, who the hell is he to tell you that your smoking killed him?

I hate this too: Even when the "critics" remain positive and respectfully suggest a new course of action for a particular program to try (such as a Bi-Bi approach), parents still freak out and say, "I don't want my child being experimented on with unproven techniques!"

As if their children aren't *already* being experimented upon with unproven techniques.

The Age of Digital Boob Magic

You see Deaf Education
can be roughly divided into
the *Baywatch* and *Knight Rider* eras
of David Hasselhoff's life.

American Sign Language was the equivalent
of a 1990s boob bouncing,
running along the beach
in slow motion

Pam Anderson lust trance.
Fat single parents of deaf children
sat on couches and flipped right over
from *Days of Our Lives*

to an entirely new kind of suntan fantasy.
Children of a Lesser God came out, and
all the books were summarily entitled
The Great Grand Blah Blah of Silence,

Hands of Gosh-Wow Wonder, and
*Their Ears Heard No Snap-Crackle-Pop
of Jesus.* Pure boob magic. No one
left the television for a century

and Deaf Education became a giant
Daniel French statue.
Then came cochlear implants
and suddenly Kit

was driving around all by itself,
no attention required.
David Hasselhoff winked, clicked,
made a few finger pistols—

you forgot he was wearing disco shirts
in the 80s because
da-dum, da-dum, da-dum
that side-to-side flashing hood light

had you hypnotized.
Harlan Lane wrote every book since.
When people got bored,
they flipped back to reruns of *Baywatch*.

Paternalism and Sleeping Cats

My cat Joe has the irritating habit of following my wife and me into the kitchen and parking himself precisely between our table and the refrigerator. It's impossible get something at dinnertime without stepping over him. I used to think he took some form of comfort from our presence, and that's why he always had to be so close to us.

Yesterday I changed that assessment.

I found myself on my hands and knees looking everywhere for him. When I couldn't find him after fifteen minutes, I began to worry. He loves to wait by the door of our apartment—when someone comes in, he goes racing out into the hallway and dashing up the steps. Had Amy accidentally let him out when she went shopping? It was raining! What if he was stuck outside, cold and wet? What if a car hit him?

I picked up my jacket to go looking for him, and there he was, sleeping snuggly against the armrest of the sofa. That's when I realized. He doesn't lie between our table and the refrigerator because he takes comfort from our presence. He does it because he knows *we* take comfort from *his*.

I wonder sometimes if parents aren't the same way with deaf children. We believe that we are the protectors, but maybe we can't accept the idea that our kids don't really need us half as much as we pretend they do. Maybe many of our deaf children deliberately avoid trying too hard in school because they sense that their independent future threatens us, that we'll go a little crazy if they do their own thing, that we'll feel somewhat frantic if they don't stay within sight.

I don't know. Somewhere there's a line that we're not supposed to cross; some point where parenting becomes more about our needs than about theirs. Until yesterday, I barely saw that line with my cat. How am I supposed to see it with my future deaf son or daughter?

Murderball

What the Deaf community needs is a documentary like *Murderball*. Seen it yet? Do! It's at Blockbuster now.

"Murderball" is actually the original name of the sport that is now called "Wheelchair Rugby." The film is about the world-class athletes who compete in the Paralympics. More or less, you take an ordinary wheelchair and reconfigure it into a battering ram. Then you find a team of players who have enough guts to fall *twice*.

Let me explain that. If you're paralyzed from the waist down, chances are you already know a little something about falling *once*. Chances are, your first fall—and by that, I don't mean your random stumble on an ice slick—snapped your spine somewhere, and now you've got a good quarter pound of metal screws holding your head up. You've probably also got a closet full of old photographs of yourself playing high school football back when you were "normal." You woke up from a six-month coma one day, endured a year or more of excruciating rehabilitation, and came home to find a newly built ramp leading to your front door. Your old bathroom has been widened so you can park your chair next to the toilet and lift yourself onto the can. And that's only if both of your arms still work.

Now take that shock, take the stress of adjustments such as those, and ask, "Okay, who's tough enough to risk that again, and more importantly, risk it all again for the sole purpose of getting a ball over a goal line?" Because when someone slams a battering-ram wheelchair into you at top speed—and friend, some of these guys can wheel those things *fast*—you are going to tip over. And if you're one of those players with only partially functioning arms, in many cases, you're not going to be able to break your fall.

I love how the movie skewers every stereotype we've ever assigned to people in wheelchairs. For example, sex: frank discussions on how to masturbate with a hand that won't fully close. There's also a few borderline X-rated segments of the wheelchair sex video many paralysis patients are shown to help answer the inevitable questions they'll have about their futures.

Another example: competitive (and not-so-competitive) violence. One player, his shoulder and leg covered in wicked tattoos, says (I'm paraphrasing), "People never know what to do when they get in fights with me. I'm going, 'What, look at the gimp in the wheelchair? Come and fucking hit me! Cuz I'm gonna hit you back!'"

He *looks* like he would hit you back, too.

Murderball is an unflinching masterpiece of empowerment. It's even got a segment from MTV's *Jackass* in which the players take turns punching the *Jackass* stuntmen in the nuts. Translation: It isn't a film that mothers of wheelchair-bound grade-schoolers would ever let them see.

Which is exactly why they need to see it.

Hearing Parents *Know!*

I keep reading in the research literature how hearing parents are adamantly insisting to everyone—from incompetent doctors to incompetent teachers to the "Deaf militants" who get up in their faces—that nobody is more qualified than they are when it comes to "knowing what's best" for their deaf children.

Okay, fair enough. But let me ask you something, you parents: If you alone know what's best for your kid, over everybody else's advice and input, solely by virtue of being Mom and Dad, why did you even bother to take him to an audiologist in the first place? Or the speech therapist or the cochlear implant specialist, for that matter? After all, you already *knew* how to handle things from the start and what the results would be, right?

I'm surprised that, with these remarkable, superior instincts of yours, you didn't simply test your kid's hearing with a funnel or something, or build his hearing aid out of old computer parts from that box in your basement. But at least now I have an explanation for why so many of you never go to ASL classes. What could such classes possibly offer *you?* You're linguistic geniuses, every last one of you, and frankly I'm ashamed of myself for even having the gall to ask whether or not you can sign to your child. Of course you can! I mean, you *know!* Who the hell am I to challenge that?

Believe it or not, I really do understand that there are parents out there who do the best they can for their kids (yes, even parents who never learn to sign). And my heart goes out to them. They're angry because incompetent doctors told them to wait another six months before having their child's hearing tested again, assuring them that everything was fine when nothing was. They're frustrated because the speech program they enrolled their kid in employs teachers who utilize a "voice-off" policy, while the signing program they enrolled their kid in employs teachers who mostly just talk. They want quality education for their children and have basically had to sue every school district in their state to make sure they got it. They're fed up, they're exhausted, they're amazingly dedicated, and they have my respect. As both an educator and a researcher, I will always give them my utmost cooperation.

But you know what? There are plenty of parents who *don't* do the best they can for their kids—not because they're grief-stricken and stuck in denial; not because they don't know how; but simply because as responsible, reasonable, capable parents, they *suck.* Think about it for a second: If there can be such a thing as incompetent doctors or incompetent teachers, why can't there be such a thing as incompetent parents? Or is that completely outside of the realm of possibility? It must be—just about every institutional review board that I know of would smack my ass with a paddle for even daring to suggest such a thing. They would sternly admonish me for my bias; my utter, reprehensible lack of objectivity! In fact I can't think of a faster way to blow my professional reputation (not to mention my prospects for continued—and future—employment) than by publicly calling hostile, destructive, and lazy parents on their bullshit.

Well hey, maybe there's a good reason for that. I mean, imagine the utter chaos that would result if doctors started assuming they knew a bit more about treating kids with cancer than their patient's parents did! Or if, dropping down to the blue-collar level for a second, licensed contractors started thinking they knew more about building a house than someone who had never picked up a hammer?

Obviously these parents took their child to an audiologist just to humor the rest of us; to keep us believing that the ivory tower is still standing and all that. Clearly we need to be careful and not overstep our bounds, here. The fact that so many deaf children graduate high school functionally illiterate obviously has no relationship to the fact that over 90 percent of them are born to selfless hearing parents who *know* what they're doing.

Maybe it's time for researchers to start acknowledging that, under the farce of objectivity and neutrality, they're enabling uninvolved parents to remain that way. It's only from a platform of moral indignation that such parents can simultaneously defend both their ignorance and their inaction.

But the only parents who truly deserve to stand there are those who tolerate neither.

Final Notes for Hearing/ Nonsigning Parents

You can more easily learn to sign than your deaf children can learn to hear. Factor this in.

* *

For safety's sake, the Deaf community should have an equal say in how deaf children are raised by hearing parents. How these parents teach their children to perceive themselves directly influences how hearing people in general come to perceive deaf people in general. Therefore if a deaf child is not taught self-esteem skills, he will become an easy target for hearing bullies who are more than happy to push him around. When he doesn't resist, these bullies understandably conclude that it should be just as easy to push all of *us* around. That's probably why there are more than a couple hearing ex-bullies walking around out there with shattered expectations and noses.

* *

For all of my misgivings about Hearing America, I do try to make a distinction between the terms *hearing* and *nonsigning.* Why condemn people for factors beyond their control? Hearing or deaf, man or woman, White or Black, heterosexual or homosexual—rejecting a person for these traits is exactly what would make me an audist, a sexist, a racist, a homophobe . . . and an idiot. In essence, I'd be getting angry over a roll of genetic dice.

I hold people accountable for the choices they make. Being a *hearing* parent isn't a choice. Being a *nonsigning* one is.

* *

Thus we come to the end of this book, and to the last message I wanted to leave you with: We all make choices. Some are harder than others, and some are worse than others. We also live with consequences. I don't talk to my parents that much, and they don't talk to me that much. On both our parts, that's a choice. I don't condemn them—I simply acknowledge reality. This didn't just happen to us by accident. It didn't just happen "one day." It happened deliberately, and it keeps happening *every* day. We both make the same choices over and over. They choose to not learn to sign, and as a result, I choose to not allow them further into my life. This, in turn, probably doesn't do a whole lot to inspire them to learn to sign. As author Frantz Fanon suggests, "The cause is the consequence."

I can tell you this, though. . . . When they make a different choice, so will I.

Do you think I'm cruel? Inflexible and disrespectful? You miss the point. *I'm* not the one you have to worry about—your kid is. And whether you like it or not, it will someday be within his power to make a choice similar to my own. Are you ready for that?

Be sure.

Afterword

The introduction to this book was completed sometime in the beginning of April 2006, approximately one month before the Unity for Gallaudet (UFG) protest began. I was tempted many times throughout the protest to change what I had written, especially in light of the way the phrase "not Deaf enough" was being used to distract the public from realities that had nothing whatsoever to do with Deaf identity politics. In the end, however, I decided to leave the introduction alone. There is such a thing, you see, as telling a lie with the truth. And there's also just plain old lying. If I can possibly get away with it, I'd really like to spend the rest of my life avoiding both.

I meant what I said in my introduction. Once upon a time the three holy criteria for deciding whether or not someone fit into the Deaf community were having deaf parents, attending a residential institution, and being able to sign grammatically perfect ASL. That's the truth, and here's another one—a lot of deaf people really were rejected for not meeting those criteria.

This was a stupid move on Deaf peoples' part because nobody has any control over what type of parents he's born to or what type of school he's initially placed in. And odds are high that if you reject someone over so-called "choices" he was never responsible for making in the first place, he's not going to think enough of you to learn your language and contribute to your culture. And without those contributions, can the culture really grow? No. Which is why—from almost as far back

221

as 1988, when Gallaudet students and staff revolted over the selection of a hearing president—it really didn't.

And what's more, now things are even worse. On more and more blogs we are seeing growing evidence of deaf on Deaf hatred. It's no longer *hearing* people calling Deaf people illiterate trailer trash or Social Security-mooching drug addicts. It's *deaf* people doing that now. It's called "blowback." "Not Deaf enough," justly or not, really is what set that whole thing off. What goes around comes around. And in many ways, that blowback is exactly what more than a few Deaf people have had coming to them for decades.

That's the truth. But this is what makes all of that a lie: I fit into the "hearing world" far better than a nonspeaking, ASL-signing, English-illiterate Deaf person ever will, and so does any D/deaf person like me. By some fluke I was born with only a mild hearing loss that later progressed to profound deafness. The result? I was able to acquire spoken English as my native language. My voice doesn't sound like a hyena's. My printed English sentences don't look like they've just been spit out of a paper shredder.

Does that sound rude? Truth often does. You tell me which type of person Hearing America is built for, which one it can more readily relate to, which one it will hire—Deaf or deaf? The fact of the matter is you don't need to tell me. This country answers those very questions every single day, and quite savagely. For every person out there who has been rejected for being not Deaf enough, there are a dozen more being rejected daily because they are *too Deaf.*

And what's more, I can milk that for all it's worth. All I have to do is distance myself from the whole "Deaf absolutist" thing, and any individual perceived of being one. In fact, all I really need to do is make that group my scapegoat. Suddenly my game plan is clear. *They* are the stupid ones—not me! They are the ones who can't read and write, who reject cochlear implants and the benefits of modern medicine because they're afraid of facing the real world. Look at me . . . see my hearing aid? See me say, "Yes, sir" and "No, sir?" Those absolutists don't represent me, no way! I'm a realist! I'm for progress! I'm for inclusion! I'm . . .

See what I mean? With enough selective truths, you really can build the perfect lie.

Now in the midst of all that, where do we stand? And more importantly, what do we do next? The Hearing/hearing and Deaf/deaf blogging world has already started exploring these questions (ironically rendering this book somewhat out of date in the process). You can scarcely read anything anymore that doesn't contain some kind of challenge to what we once pretended were perfectly valid ways to be deaf. The quality, the integrity, the very *legitimacy* of educational programs for deaf people all across this nation are being questioned (some would say attacked) as never before. UFG woke our community up to the fact that things have to change. It made our community realize just how many people are fed up with trying to work within the system. Indeed, during those final few tumultuous weeks of October 2006, it became starkly clear just how many people were ready to destroy that system if they had to—even if doing so meant destroying the institution itself.

So, what *do* we do next? My editor asked me to provide some of my own insights into this question at the end of *Bug*, rather than leave the task to the blogs. The request was hardly unjustified. Any book that uses the bulk of its content to rip apart old answers owes its readers some new ones. To tell you the truth, during the UFG protest, quite a few people asked me to do the same thing. I remember one such incident very clearly. It was the night the Gallaudet University Board of Trustees left the campus after reaffirming their support for Dr. Fernandes as the ninth president of Gallaudet. The students had locked down Hall Memorial Building (HMB) all day, and they held a meeting almost as soon as the board's email went out to the campus community. Several student leaders asked their fellow protesters what they wanted to do: stay in HMB and continue to lock it down, or leave and continue the fight in some other way?

My memory is a bit fuzzy regarding subsequent events. Everyone ended up splitting into groups, with the faculty going off to one room, the staff going to another, and the students staying in the atrium. I don't remember what my colleagues decided. I felt—and I still feel—like I had aged twenty years in the last six months. I was utterly emotionally exhausted. I think everyone was.

I do, however, clearly remember what happened after the group meetings. We all walked back to the atrium, where the student leaders asked us to vote with our feet. Many of the people standing in the atrium, including me, were not among those who had locked down the building earlier that morning. We had come in to meet with the students after we learned of what had happened (especially because no interpreters had been provided to facilitate communication between the students and campus security, and tensions between those two groups had been high for quite some time). Those in the crowd who wished to stay and continue occupying HMB were asked to walk to the right side of the atrium. Those who wanted to leave and continue protesting in some other manner were asked to walk to the left.

A young woman who had been standing near one of the pillars then approached me. She may have been a student—I don't know. I had only seen her a few times before. I haven't seen her since.

She asked me what I thought she should do. I didn't know how to answer. In my exhaustion I remember thinking, *Why ask me? Why is it my responsibility to tell you what to do? That's why we're stuck in all of this shit; everyone keeps waiting around for someone else to tell them what to do!*

I didn't sign this to her, though. I had run out of the energy to remain angry. Yet strangely enough, I did have the energy to remain hopeful. I felt an earnest desire for all of us to go on somehow, to make it through this and survive as a community, albeit a far more honest one than we had been previously. But to do this, we had to face ourselves and, for once, answer only to ourselves. Why? Because you can't have anything if you don't have yourself. It is not just your culture (and those who oppress your culture) that instills you with values. It's a two-way street. Through your actions and inactions you create the values of your culture. You create its will to resist just as surely as you create its apathy, its surrender. Thus, you can never make the argument that nobody is listening to you if you don't even know what the hell it is you want. You can't stand up for what you think is right until you can decide for yourself exactly what is wrong.

But because the instillation of values is a two-way street— from your culture to you and vice-versa—we also have to allow for the fact that, sometimes, waiting around for someone to tell us what to do isn't about fear and apathy. Sometimes it's about actually trying to respect our community. After all, isn't that what others ceaselessly berate us for every time we try to stand up and do something? We should respect those around us and not stomp on their dreams and aspirations, their sense of self, just so we can plow ahead in defense of what we know is right? Maybe our hesitation in some moments actually *is* about heeding that criticism and honoring the concept of "appreciation for diverse views."

So it could be that the young woman wasn't asking me to tell her what to do at all. Maybe she was trying to get me to tell her what *I* was going to do, so she could make her own decision with respect for mine. Then again, maybe that was just wishful thinking on my part. Who knows? In times of great stress, it feels nice to believe. I put one hand on her shoulder and gave it a reassuring squeeze. With an apologetic shrug, I used my free hand to reply, "Do what you think is right." For a brief moment she looked puzzled, and then her expression changed to resigned understanding.

I gave her a hug and made my choice.

That was then . . . this is now, and here we are. Once again, someone is asking me what we should do next. But you already know what I'm going to say, don't you? You have to come up with your own answers. All I can do after this point is wish you luck in your search for them.

A word of warning, though—call it one for the road. The answers you come up with at first will be the answers you are ready to face. So on those sorrowful days when, in retrospect, you realize that you lost something because you weren't ready to face a particular answer, learn from that. Learn from that bitter lesson, friend, because if you truly want to evolve, that knowledge is the only thing that can lead you to what you really have to accept—you were never ready to face the question.